ULTIMATE
FOOTBALL HEROES

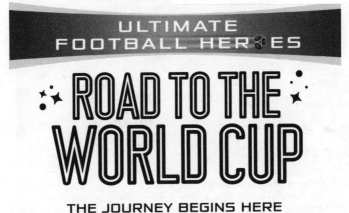

ROAD TO THE
WORLD CUP

THE JOURNEY BEGINS HERE

DINO

Published by Dino Books
an imprint of John Blake Publishing
3 Bramber Court, 2 Bramber Road,
London W14 9PB, England

www.johnblakepublishing.co.uk

www.facebook.com/johnblakebooks 🇫
twitter.com/jblakebooks 🇪

This edition published in 2018

ISBN: 978 1 78606 920 7

British Library Cataloguing-in-Publication Data:

A catalogue record for this book is available from the British Library.

Design by www.envydesign.co.uk

Printed and bound in Great Britain by Clays Ltd, St Ives plc

1 3 5 7 9 10 8 6 4 2

Papers used by John Blake Publishing are natural, recyclable products made from
wood grown in sustainable forests. The manufacturing processes conform to the
environmental regulations of the country of origin.

Every attempt has been made to contact the relevant copyright-holders, but some
were unobtainable. We would be grateful if the appropriate people could contact us.

John Blake Publishing is an imprint of Bonnier Publishing.
www.bonnierpublishing.co.uk

For Noah and Nico,
Southampton's future strikeforce

ULTIMATE
FOOTBALL HEROES

Matt Oldfield is an accomplished writer and the editor-in-chief
of football review site *Of Pitch & Page*. Tom Oldfield is a freelance
sports writer and the author of biographies on Cristiano Ronaldo,
Arsène Wenger and Rafael Nadal.

Cover illustration by Dan Leydon.
To learn more about Dan visit danleydon.com
To purchase his artwork visit etsy.com/shop/footynews
Or just follow him on Twitter @danleydon

TABLE OF CONTENTS

ACKNOWLEDGEMENTS

First of all, I'd like to thank John Blake Publishing –
and particularly my editor James Hodgkinson – for
giving me the opportunity to work on these books
and for supporting me throughout. Writing stories for
the next generation of football fans is both an honour
and a pleasure.

I wouldn't be doing this if it wasn't for my brother
Tom. I owe him so much and I'm very grateful for
his belief in me as an author. I feel like Robin setting
out on a solo career after a great partnership with
Batman. I hope I do him (Tom, not Batman) justice
with these new books.

Next up, I want to thank my friends for keeping

me sane during long hours in front of the laptop. Pang, Will, Mills, Doug, John, Charlie – the laughs and the cups of coffee are always appreciated.

I've already thanked my brother but I'm also very grateful to the rest of my family, especially Melissa, Noah and of course Mum and Dad. To my parents, I owe my biggest passions: football and books. They're a real inspiration for everything I do.

Finally, I couldn't have done this without Iona's encouragement and understanding during long, work-filled weekends. Much love to you.

RONALDO

PART ONE

EUROPEAN GLORY

Stade de France, 10 July 2016

Cristiano had already won so many trophies during his amazing career – one La Liga title with Real Madrid, three Premier League titles with Manchester United, three Champions League trophies and three Ballon d'Ors. But there was still something missing. That something was an international trophy with Portugal.

'The best footballers always lead their countries to glory,' Cristiano told his best friend Nani. 'I'm one of the best and I need to prove it!'

As he walked out onto the pitch in Paris, Cristiano was one step away from achieving his dream. With his confidence and three crucial goals during the Euro

2016 championship, he had led his team all the way to the final. At the Stade de France, Portugal faced a France team with home advantage and world-class players like Paul Pogba and Antoine Griezmann.

After beating the World Champions Germany in the semi-finals, France were the favourites to win. Portugal were the underdogs, but they had the best player in Europe – Cristiano – and he had never been more determined to win.

Once their coach, Fernando Santos, had finished his team talk in the dressing room, it was time for the senior players to speak. Nani went first and then it was the captain's turn.

'We've done so well to get this far,' Cristiano told his teammates, 'but let's not settle for second place. We can do this! One more win and we will go down in history. One more win and we will return home as heroes!'

The whole squad cheered. Together, they believed that they could become the champions of Europe.

Cristiano stood with his eyes closed for the Portuguese national anthem. He didn't mumble the words under his breath; he shouted them at the top of his voice. He was pumped up and ready to do his country proud on the pitch.

After seven minutes, Cristiano got the ball just inside the French half. As he turned to attack, Dimitri Payet rushed in with a heavy challenge.

'Foul!' the Portugal fans cried out as Cristiano fell to the floor.

When the referee waved play on, everyone expected Cristiano to get back up, but he didn't. He couldn't. He stayed down on the ground, holding his left knee and screaming in agony.

Oww!

Cristiano wasn't faking; this was a serious injury. As the physios used the magic spray and rubbed his knee with an ice pack, he winced. He put his hands to his face to hide his tears.

Up in the stands, there was panic on the face of every Portugal fan. Could they win the final without their superstar? They didn't think so. When Cristiano stood up and limped over to the touchline, they clapped and cheered.

'Don't give up – we need you, CR7!'

Cristiano tested his leg – it didn't feel good, but he had to keep playing.

'Are you sure?' João Mário asked him as he walked back onto the pitch.

'I have to try!' Cristiano told him.

But a minute later, he collapsed to the ground again. On his big day, Cristiano was in too much pain to continue. He kept shaking his head. He couldn't believe his bad luck.

'You have to go off,' Nani said, giving his friend a hug. 'We'll do our skipper proud, I promise!'

Cristiano still wasn't ready to leave the field, though. It was his dream to play in a Euro final and he wasn't giving up yet. The physios put a bandage around his knee and he went back on. Third time lucky he hoped, but when he tried to run, he had to stop. Reluctantly, he signalled to the bench: 'I need to come off.'

Cristiano ripped off his captain's armband. 'Wear this,' he said to Nani, 'and win this final!'

'Don't worry, skipper, we'll win for you!' Pepe shouted.

As he was carried off on a stretcher, Cristiano cried and cried. The most important match of his life was over before it had properly begun.

But Cristiano didn't hide away, feeling sorry for himself. He was still Portugal's captain and now that he wasn't on the pitch, his teammates needed him more than ever.

At half-time, Cristiano was there in the dressing room, urging his team on. 'Stick together and keep fighting!' he told them. It was still 0–0 – there was everything to play for.

In the second half, Cristiano was there on the bench, biting his fingernails and, in his head, kicking every ball. Watching his Portugal team play without him was like torture, but what else could he do? He had to do something to help.

Just before striker Eder went on as a sub, Cristiano looked him in the eyes and said, 'Be strong. You're going to score the winner, I know it.'

But after ninety minutes, it was still 0–0. Cristiano hobbled around giving encouragement to the tired players. 'Keep going, lads. You can do this!'

After 109 minutes, Eder got the ball, shrugged off the French defender and sent a rocket of a shot into the bottom corner.

Goooooooooooooooaaaaaaaaaaaaaaaaaaalllllllllllllll llllllllllll!!!!!!!!!!!!!!!!!!!!!!!!!

Cristiano went wild. He jumped out of his seat and threw his arms in the air. It hurt to jump up and down, but in that amazing moment, he didn't care. The other subs rushed onto the field to celebrate with Eder, but Cristiano was in too much pain for that. Instead, he just kept punching the air with joy. They were so close to victory now.

For the last ten minutes, he stood with Santos as Portugal's second manager. He limped along the touchline, pointing and shouting instructions to the players.

Run! Defend! Take your time!

When the whistle finally went, Cristiano let out a howl of happiness as the tears rolled down his cheeks again. He hugged each and every one of his incredible teammates and thanked them.

'I told you we'd do it!' Pepe laughed.

Cristiano took his shirt off and threw it into the crowd. The Portugal coaches had to find him a new one so that he could do his captain's duty – collecting the Euro 2016 trophy.

He climbed the steps slowly, giving high-fives to all the fans he passed. The trophy was decorated with red and green ribbons, the colours of Portugal's flag. As Cristiano lifted the trophy, the whole team cheered behind him. He kissed it and then passed it on to the other players. No words could describe the joy that Cristiano was feeling.

But he was never satisfied for long. Cristiano was always looking ahead to his next challenge, his next final, his next trophy. That's what made him such a superstar.

'You know what comes after Euro 2016, don't you?' Cristiano said with that famous fire in his eyes. 'The 2018 World Cup!'

PART TWO

PORTUGAL'S MAIN MAN

When the Portugal players saw the 2018 World Cup qualification draw, most of them were delighted. In Group B, they would face…

…Switzerland…

…Hungary…

…Faroe Islands…

…Latvia…

…and Andorra.

It didn't look too tricky, but as captain, Cristiano wasn't taking anything for granted.

'Do you remember the qualification for Brazil 2014?' he said to Nani and Pepe. 'We thought we had a good group then too, but Russia won it and we had to beat Sweden in the play-offs. I don't want a repeat of that this time!'

Cristiano was desperate to show the world that Euro 2016 wasn't a fluke. Portugal were a top team, capable of beating anyone, but they couldn't relax. Quite the opposite; they had to work harder than ever to improve.

Cristiano's knee injury meant that he missed the first match away in Switzerland. This time, without their main man, Portugal collapsed to a 2–0 defeat. After the high of winning Euro 2016, they had crashed back down to earth. The players were all very disappointed.

'That was only our first match and our toughest match too,' Cristiano told his teammates calmly. There was no need to panic yet. 'We just need to win the rest now!'

Portugal's main man was back for the next match against Andorra, and he was back with a bang. With four minutes gone, Cristiano had already scored twice and was aiming for a hat-trick. He celebrated each goal with his cool new 'Right Here,

Right Now' jump and spin. The Portugal fans
loved it.

Ronaldo! Ronaldo! Ronaldo!

Just after half-time, André Gomes turned in the
box and fired a low ball across to Cristiano. It was
a difficult chance, but he made it look so easy. With
perfect technique, Cristiano guided the ball in on the
volley.

*Goooooooooooooooooooooaaaaaaaaaaaaaaaaallllllll
llllllllllllllllll!!!!!!!!!!!!!!!!!!!*

A hat-trick on his return! Cristiano ran straight
over to André Gomes.

'Great pass!' he said, giving him a high-five and
a hug.

Cristiano still wasn't finished. He added a fourth
goal, and Portugal won 6–0. Three days later, the
Faroe Islands received the same six-goal treatment.
This time, Cristiano only scored once, and young
striker André Silva was the hat-trick hero. All three
were tap-ins, but that didn't matter at all.

Cristiano was one of the first players to run
over and congratulate André Silva. 'I like your style,'

he said with a smile. 'You're a proper poacher!'

For years, Portugal had been missing a top-class striker. Cristiano had played the role at Euro 2016, but with André Silva doing so well up front, he could now play a little deeper. He loved the freedom of his new role. With more time and space on the ball, he could create lots of chances.

Against Latvia, Nani and Cristiano played a great one-two. As Nani burst into the box, he was tripped by the defender. Penalty! Cristiano made no mistake from the spot.

Goooooooooooooooooooooooaaaaaaaaaaaaaaaaaa allllllllllllllllllllllll!!!!!!!!!!!

In the second half, Cristiano stepped up to take another penalty to make it 2–0. He aimed for the bottom corner, but the ball hit the post, then the goalkeeper, and bounced away from danger.

'No way!' Cristiano shouted angrily.

How had that not gone in? He hated making mistakes. Ten minutes later, Latvia scored a surprise equaliser. Suddenly, Portugal had work to do.

As captain, Cristiano stayed calm. 'Just keep doing

what you're doing!' he called out to André Silva
and Ricardo Quaresma. 'We'll get another goal, no
problem.'

In the end, they scored another three goals and
won 4–1. Manager Fernando Santos was pleased
with his team's fightback.

'But next time,' he told them afterwards, 'don't let
them score in the first place!'

Cristiano's amazing 2016 ended with more
silverware in Paris. He beat Lionel Messi to win his
fourth Ballon d'Or. What a year it had been – 48
goals in 52 games, the Champions League *and* Euro
2016 trophies.

'Thank you very much,' Cristiano said in French as
he lifted the big golden ball. It felt like it belonged in
his hands.

'It's an unbelievable moment for me,' he
continued in English. 'I'm so proud. Thank you to
everyone who voted for me and thank you to all my
teammates – for Real Madrid and for the Portugal
national team!'

Cristiano enjoyed his big night, but he went

straight back to work afterwards. He wanted to win a fifth Ballon d'Or, then a sixth. To do that, he needed to make sure that every year was as successful as 2016. There was one big trophy that he was desperate to win – the 2018 World Cup.

To do that, Cristiano's partnership with André Silva needed to keep on firing. Next up: Hungary. At Euro 2016, Cristiano had scored two goals in an entertaining 3–3 draw. Nine months on, however, it was a totally different contest, thanks to Portugal's new star strikeforce.

After thirty minutes, Cristiano dribbled through the Hungary midfield and passed to Raphaël Guerreiro on the left. His first-time cross found André Silva at the back post for another simple tap-in. 1–0!

Portugal were playing brilliant football and it was about to get even better. As a long ball floated towards him, André Silva had an idea. Instead of shooting, he flicked it cleverly back to his partner. Cristiano was on to it in a flash. With one touch, he smashed the ball into the bottom corner.

*Goooooooooooooooooooooooaaaaaaaaaalllllllllllllll
llllllllllllll!!!!!!!!!!!!!!!!!!!*

Cristiano pointed over at André Silva and smiled.
The team spirit was higher than ever. 'Nice skill,
mate,' he said. 'Thanks!'

In the second half, Portugal won a free kick on
the left side. There was no question about who
would take it. Cristiano stared down at the ball
and took a long, deep breath. He was feeling even
more confident than usual. 'This is going in!' he told
himself. His shot dipped and swerved, past the wall,
and then past the goalkeeper too.

*Goooooooooooooooooooooooaaaaaaaaaaaaaaaalll
llllllllllllllllll!!!!!!!!!!!!!!!*

Pepe jumped up on his back. 'Seriously, what
would we do without you?' he asked.

Cristiano shrugged. He had scored nine goals in his
last four games. There was just no stopping Portugal's
main man.

PART THREE

MORE, MORE, MORE

Unfortunately, there was no stopping Switzerland either. With five wins out of five, they were still three points clear at the top of Group B.

'All we can do is keep winning,' Cristiano told his teammates. In the back of his mind, he was already looking ahead to their final qualifier – the return match against Switzerland.

But before that, Portugal were off to Latvia. It was the end of the club season and Cristiano was feeling a mixture of happiness and exhaustion. He had won another Champions League trophy with Real Madrid, and they had also beaten their rivals Barcelona to the La Liga title.

'Revenge is sweet!' he laughed with his club teammate Marcelo.

Cristiano was the best big game player around. When his team needed him most, he came alive. He scored a hat-trick against Atlético Madrid in the Champions League semi-finals, and then two more goals in the final against Juventus.

Now, six days later, it was time for Cristiano to be the hero for his country. Portugal were relying on him, but as the minutes went by, it looked like he might not have any goals left in his tired legs.

Cristiano dribbled infield and unleashed a powerful long-range shot. What a great save from the keeper!

Cristiano turned on the edge of the penalty area and aimed for the bottom corner. Another great save from the keeper!

'Why can't I score?' Cristiano screamed, kicking the air in frustration.

Bruno Alves put an arm around his shoulder. 'You're trying too hard, mate. We don't need you to score a special goal – just a goal of any kind!'

José Fonte hit the post and the ball bounced down

in the six-yard box. Cristiano was the first to react. At the back post, his diving header got the ball over the line.

Goooooooooooooooooooooaaaaaaaaaaaaaaaaalllllllll lllllllllllll!!!!!!!!!!!!!!!!!!!!!

Cristiano's second was a simple tap-in too.

'Not your prettiest goal, mate!' Bruno Alves joked as they celebrated.

Cristiano was on a hat-trick yet again. He always wanted more, more, more, but he was learning not to be quite so selfish. As Portugal's experienced captain, it was his job to lead the talented new generation of players like André Gomes, André Silva, Bernardo Silva and Renato Sanches.

Cristiano was pleased with their progress. He gave them lots of advice in training and he trusted them on the pitch. To win as a team, they had to play as a team. When the ball came to him on the edge of the penalty area, Cristiano passed across to André Silva. 3–0!

'Thanks!' André Silva cheered, running over to high-five his amazing strike partner.

Cristiano needed a summer holiday but that would have to wait. As the winners of Euro 2016, Portugal were off to Russia to play in the 2017 Confederations Cup. If there was a trophy up for grabs, Cristiano could never say no.

'This is the warm-up for the main event next year,' he told his teammates. 'Let's show everyone that we're good enough to win the World Cup!'

To make it through to the semi-finals, Portugal needed to beat New Zealand. Cristiano scored a penalty, but it was the Silvas who stole the show. Bernardo got the second goal and André got the third. They were playing so well that Fernando Santos was able to rest Cristiano for the last thirty minutes.

'What? Why are you taking me off?' he cried out.

Cristiano was never satisfied, but Portugal needed their main man to be on top form for the semi-final. He did his best to create more magic but there was no way through the Chile defence. The match went to penalties.

Cristiano did what he always did. 'I'll take the fifth one,' he told his manager.

Going last gave Cristiano the chance to be the hero, but only if his teammates scored before him. Ricardo Quaresma, João Moutinho and Nani all missed, and Cristiano didn't even get to take his penalty.

'Unlucky, guys,' he said, comforting his disappointed teammates. 'That was just the rehearsal – remember, it's all about the 2018 World Cup!'

Cristiano finally got the relaxing break that he needed, but he soon grew restless. What was life without football? He never got tired of winning. He always wanted more, more, more. He couldn't wait to get back into international action against the Faroe Islands.

'Come on, let's keep up the pressure!' he urged André Silva before kick-off.

In the first few minutes, Bernardo Silva crossed towards Cristiano at the back post. The ball was slightly behind him, so Cristiano had to think fast. He leapt into the air and went for an acrobatic scissor-kick.

Goooooooooooooooooooooooooaaaaaaaaaaaaaaaalllllll lllllllllllllllllllllllll!!!!!!!!!!

What a strike, what a start! As Cristiano ran towards the corner flag, he pointed to himself,

'Right here!'

and then down at the pitch...

'Right now!'

The fans loved his famous celebration. They couldn't get enough of it, no matter how many goals he scored.

Ronaldo! Ronaldo! Ronaldo!

After sixty-five minutes, Cristiano had his hat-trick and Portugal had the victory they needed. The players could focus on their next game away in Hungary. They knew it wouldn't be so straight-forward.

'We just need to be patient,' Fernando Santos told his players in the dressing room. 'We've got the best attackers in the world – we'll score!'

Cristiano would make sure of that. With seventy-eight international goals, he was now ahead of his idol Pelé, but he still wanted more, more, more. He cut in from the left wing and took a swerving shot at goal. The Hungary goalkeeper did well to tip it over the bar.

Cristiano turned away and slapped his leg. 'So close!' he screamed at the sky.

For once, it just wasn't Cristiano's day in front of goal but that didn't stop him playing a vital role for Portugal. He was born to make a difference.

Just after half-time, Cristiano ran onto João Moutinho's through-ball. He was on the left side of the penalty area with four Hungary defenders between him and the goal. But at the back post, he spotted André Silva on the move. With a lovely chipped cross, Cristiano picked him out.

Goooooooooooooooooooooooooaaaaaaaaaaaaaaaaaal llllllllllllllllll!!!!!!!!!!!!!!!

Finally, Portugal had the breakthrough. The whole team celebrated together.

'Right, now keep it tight!' Cristiano shouted, playing the captain's role.

Portugal held on for another victory, but it still left them second in Group B. Cristiano had been right all along. They were heading for a huge final showdown against Switzerland. The winners would be going to the World Cup. The losers would have to wait and see. Cristiano loved a big game; he couldn't wait.

PART FOUR

READY

In his pre-game Instagram photo, Cristiano was messing around with Pepe in training. Portugal's stars looked happy and relaxed. There was a one-word message with the picture – 'Ready'.

Cristiano was born ready. Away in Andorra, he had watched the first half from the substitutes' bench. He was one yellow card away from a suspension, and his manager Fernando Santos didn't want to take the risk. Portugal were expected to win comfortably but without their main man, they were struggling. At half-time, it was still 0-0.

'Get ready, you're coming on,' Santos told him reluctantly.

Cristiano's face lit up. In a flash, the atmosphere in the dressing room lifted. Everything was going to be okay.

'Do us proud!' Pepe said, handing back the captain's armband.

Cristiano was itching to get out there and score for his country. It only took him twenty minutes. João Mário's cross eventually found its way to Cristiano. He was like a ball magnet. He controlled it and calmly slotted it home.

Goooooooooooooooooooooooaaaaaaaaaaaaaallllllll llllllllllllllllllllllll!!!!!!!!!!!!

'Ronaldo to the rescue!' André Silva cried out as he jumped on Cristiano's back.

Now, just three days later, they were about to take on Switzerland for a place at the 2018 World Cup. If Portugal won, the two nations would be on the same points, but Portugal's goal difference was much better, thanks to Cristiano and André Silva.

Nearly 60,000 Portuguese fans filled the Estádio da Luz in Lisbon to cheer on their team. Millions more were watching the match on TV across the country.

'It all comes down to this, guys,' Cristiano said in his captain's team-talk. 'We can't let our country down tonight. I don't want to end up in the play-offs again!'

As they walked out on to the pitch, the Portugal players looked up at a sea of red and green. The atmosphere was electric.

'Let's do this!' Cristiano called out before kick-off, giving a high-five to each and every teammate.

Some of the younger players looked nervous, but their captain had plenty of confidence to share. He was ready to lead by example.

André Silva had Portugal's first good chance, and Bernardo Silva had the second. Cristiano kept looking for space but every time he got the ball, there was a wall of Swiss players in front of him.

Just when Cristiano was starting to get annoyed, Eliseu delivered a dangerous cross into the box. João Mário couldn't quite reach it but it caused a moment of confusion in the Swiss defence. Out of nothing, the ball was in the net. 1–0!

'Yes!' Cristiano cheered, throwing his arms up in the air.

The Estádio da Luz erupted with noise. Portugal had just taken one giant leap towards Russia, but would one goal be enough? Cristiano didn't think so.

'Come on, let's score another!' he told his teammates.

João Moutinho played a neat one-two with Bernardo Silva on the right side of the Switzerland box. As Bernardo Silva looked up for the cross, he could see Cristiano and João Mário, but they were both being tightly marked. At the back post, André Silva was free. If Bernardo Silva could thread the pass through to him, he would score for sure.

Goooooooooooooooooooooooooaaaaaaaaaaaaaaaaal lllllllllllllllllllll!!!!!!!!!!!!!!

'What a sensational team goal!' the TV commentator shouted.

This time, Cristiano wasn't Portugal's hero, but that didn't matter. What mattered was that they were off to the World Cup together.

'Great work!' he cried out at the final whistle, hugging each and every player.

Cristiano walked around the pitch, smiling and

clapping the brilliant supporters. They had played a key role in Portugal's winning performance.

'Great team effort! Russia, here we come!' he posted on Instagram later that night.

It was a relief to qualify but Portugal still had lots more hard work ahead of them. At the 2014 tournament in Brazil, they had crashed out in the group stage. They had to do better this time.

Cristiano believed in his team. He was still Portugal's main man. He had shown it time and time again, with fifteen goals in only nine games. Only Poland's Robert Lewandowski had scored more than him in qualification. In big matches with the pressure on, you could never rule Cristiano out.

But he wasn't Portugal's only star anymore. The team had a winning combination of experience and excitement. André Silva, Bernardo Silva and André Gomes were all talented young players who could help Cristiano to lift that one big trophy he was missing – the World Cup.

POGBA

PART ONE

EUROPEAN HEARTBREAK

Stade de France, 10 July 2016

The Euro 2016 final was over – France 0 Portugal 1. As Cristiano Ronaldo went wild with his teammates, Paul stood there on the pitch, alone and in shock. Had that really just happened?

France had been the clear favourites to win. Their team was playing brilliantly. Captain Hugo Lloris was making amazing saves in goal, Paul was playing awesome passes in midfield and Antoine Griezmann was on fire in attack. They had beaten World Champions Germany in the semi-final, and they were playing on home soil. What could go wrong?

The Stade de France was covered in the national

colours – blue, white and red. The atmosphere was incredible until the 109th minute. That's when Eder scored the goal that broke French hearts. With the whole country expecting victory, their dream final had turned into a nightmare. Cristiano had gone off injured early on, and they still couldn't score against Portugal.

'How did we lose that?' Paul asked himself. He lifted his shirt over his face to hide his tears.

After a few minutes, his teammate Patrice Evra came over and put an arm around his shoulder. 'Hey, we did our best out there. It just wasn't our night. You'll be back and next time, you'll win!'

Paul always listened to his 'Uncle Pat'. They had known each other for years, ever since Paul was the star of the Manchester United youth team and Patrice was the first-team left-back. Whenever Paul had a bad game or missed home, 'Uncle Pat' was always there to help and offer advice. But at the age of thirty-five, this would be Patrice's last international tournament.

'I know, but I wanted to win the Euros with

you, and I wanted to win it *here*,' Paul muttered, looking up into the stands above them. Most of the disappointed French fans had already gone home.

The Stade de France was where Paul's childhood hero, Zinedine Zidane, had won the 1998 World Cup for his country. Thanks to his two amazing headers, France had beaten Ronaldo's Brazil. Paul still remembered watching the final on TV in Renardière with his brothers, aged five. Eighteen years later, he had hoped to be his country's hero against the other Ronaldo, Portugal's Cristiano.

'Next time,' Paul told himself.

He wanted to escape straight down the tunnel, but instead he did the right thing and stayed on the pitch. To be a great winner, he had to be a great loser too. Paul shook hands with all the Portugal players. He went up on the stage to collect his silver runner-up medal, but it didn't stay around his neck for long.

'Gold is the only medal that I'm interested in,' he told Anthony Martial as they walked away.

Back in the silent dressing room, Antoine looked

even more upset than Paul. He had missed a few good chances in the final and he blamed himself.

'No man, this is a team!' Paul said, hugging his friend. 'We win together, and we lose together.'

Once all the players were sitting down, their manager Didier Deschamps spoke to them.

'Right now, you're disappointed, devastated. I understand. You've worked really hard and I'm proud of you all. But in a couple of months, our next challenge begins. Let's learn our lessons from tonight and go and win the 2018 World Cup!'

In fact, their road to the World Cup began even earlier than that. Just two weeks after the Euro 2016 final, the qualification group draw took place in Russia. France would be playing in Group A against...

Netherlands...

Sweden...

Bulgaria...

Belarus...

and Luxembourg.

The top team in each group would qualify

automatically for the World Cup and the runner-up would go into the play-offs.

'I'm happy with that draw,' Paul told Antoine when they saw France's opponents. 'There's no-one we can't beat. Russia here we come!'

PART TWO

POGBOOM

France's road to the World Cup kicked off with a difficult away trip to Belarus. Paul was determined to help his country. After losing the Euro 2016 final, it was important for them to get off to a good start in Group A.

At club level, Paul was now a Manchester United player again. Not only that but he was also the most expensive footballer in the world: £89million – there was even more pressure on him to shine.

Antoine dribbled at the defence and then slid a pass across to Paul. He was in the middle of the pitch, thirty yards from goal – the perfect position for 'Agent P'. The French fans held their breath...

His strike dipped and swerved through the air but in the end, it was an easy save for the goalkeeper. That didn't put Paul off, though. His long-range shooting was so good that they called him 'Pogboom'.

'I just need more power next time,' he told himself.

After forty-five minutes, the score was still 0–0. France needed a moment of magic. When Paul got the ball outside the penalty area, the Belarus midfielders expected him to shoot again. But instead, Paul chipped a beautiful, no-look pass into Antoine's path. Antoine ran into the box and jumped high, but the ball flew just over his head. So close!

'Great idea!' he shouted, giving Paul the thumbs-up.

France had chance after chance, but they just couldn't score. When the referee blew the final whistle, it felt as disappointing as a defeat.

'At least we got one point,' Paul told Antoine as they trudged off the pitch together. 'Don't worry, we're just finding our feet.'

France hoped that a home game would help, but it didn't look that way when their opponents Bulgaria scored an early penalty. The Stade de France fell silent – it was like the Euro 2016 Final all over again.

'Come on, we've got plenty of time to win this!' Paul told his teammates.

He never stopped believing. By half-time, France were winning 3–1, thanks to goals from Kevin Gameiro, Dimitri Payet and Antoine.

'That's more like it!' Paul cheered, hugging his friend.

He was pleased with the team victory, but it was yet another game without a goal for Paul. He was starting to worry.

'I really need to find my shooting boots again,' he admitted to Antoine. 'I used to score all the time at Juventus, but I've only got one goal for United so far. What's happened to me? For France, I've only scored one goal in three years!'

'Don't worry, I'll always make up for your poor shooting!' Antoine joked. 'But seriously, scoring goals isn't your only role in the team, Paul. You're our pass-master in midfield. You win the ball and create chances for the rest of us. We'd be lost without you in the middle!'

Paul smiled. It was nice to hear that from his

teammate. He would have lots of other opportunities to be France's hero, starting with their next big match against the Netherlands.

Paul had been looking forward to the game for months. The Dutch team wasn't as good as it used to be, but they still had top players like Arjen Robben, Kevin Strootman and Paul's Manchester United teammates Daley Blind and Memphis Depay.

'Bring it on, I can't wait to beat you guys!' Paul teased them during club training sessions. 'But don't worry – I promise I'll swap shirts with one of you at the end.'

Now, Paul had to back up those confident words. He needed to step up and lead France to victory. There was a lot of responsibility resting on his shoulders, for both club and country, but Paul was determined to prove himself as a big-game player.

After thirty minutes, Laurent Koscielny intercepted a pass and played the ball forward to Dimitri. Dimitri knew exactly where Paul would be – in the middle, within shooting range.

Pogba! Pogba! Pogba!

The French fans urged Paul to shoot. He didn't let them down. He took one touch to control the ball and then fired a powerful strike at goal.

Pogboom!

Maarten Stekelenburg thought he could save Paul's shot, but as the ball flew towards him, it suddenly dipped and swerved away from him. In the end, the Dutch goalkeeper could only tip the ball into the corner of the net.

Goooooooooooooooooooooooaaaaaaaaaaaaaaaaaallllll llllllllllllllllllllllll!!!!!!!!!!!!!

What a rocket! Paul didn't rush towards the fans to celebrate. He didn't move, or even smile. He just stood there, nodding his head as if to say, 'See, that's what I can do!'

His teammates sprinted over to congratulate him. Raphaël Varane jumped up on Paul's back. 'What a strike!' he cheered.

Pogboom was France's hero. His wondergoal turned out to be the matchwinner. It was a very proud moment, but there wasn't time to relax for long.

'We've got one more match in 2016,' Deschamps

told his players. 'If we win, we'll stay top of the group. That's where we need to be. Let's finish this year on a high!'

France's opponent at the Stade de France was Sweden. They were a well-organised team, but they had lost their star player, Paul's friend and Manchester United teammate, Zlatan Ibrahimović.

'I wish you hadn't retired from international football,' Paul told Zlatan in training. 'I was looking forward to beating you!'

'Never,' Zlatan replied with an evil grin.

After his goal against the Netherlands, Paul was feeling confident. He had the taste for it now, and he wanted to score more. Paul passed to Olivier and burst forward for the one-two. His first touch was good, but he totally fluffed his shot.

'Come on, you can do better than that!' Paul criticised himself.

A few minutes later, he curled a shot just over the crossbar.

'Unlucky! You're getting closer,' Antoine encouraged him.

Even when Sweden took the lead, Paul stayed focused. As Dimitri crossed the free kick into the box, Paul and Raphaël both jumped for the header. The ball hit the underside of the crossbar and dropped down in the net.

Goooooooooooooooooooooooaaaaaaaaaaaaaaaaaalllll lllllllllllllllllllllllll!!!!!!!!!!!!!

But whose goal was it? Both players celebrated as if they had scored. Half of the France team ran to Paul and half ran to Raphaël.

'Who got the last touch?' Antoine asked Paul.

'Me! That's definitely my goal,' he replied, as they ran back for the restart. 'But who cares? The main thing is we scored!'

A few minutes later, Dimitri got the winner for France. Three wins and a draw – that was a pretty good start.

After the match, Paul posted a photo of his goal celebration on Instagram. Pumping his fist, he looked strong and determined. Nothing would stop him from achieving his World Cup dream.

PART THREE

FRIENDS UNITED

'Go France!' Paul wrote on Instagram with a picture of the national team badge.

Due to a hamstring injury, he had to miss the next World Cup qualifier against Luxembourg. He hated not playing, but he trusted his teammates to do a good job without him. Back at his home in Manchester, he cheered for each goal in the 3–1 win.

'I'll be #PogBack soon!' Paul promised his fans.

He was back in plenty of time for France's next matches in June. However, by then, Paul wasn't feeling as fighting fit as normal. He was at the end of a long and successful first season back at Manchester United.

Nine goals in fifty-one games – there was certainly room for improvement but winning the League Cup and the Europa League wasn't a bad way to begin. Now, Paul's tired legs needed a rest. Just two weeks earlier, he had scored in the Europa League Final against Ajax.

'After these games, I'm off to chill out for a bit!' he told their goalkeeper, and captain, Hugo Lloris. He couldn't wait.

With seconds left against Sweden, the score was 1–1. A draw was a decent result away from home, especially as they weren't playing very well.

But as the referee put the whistle to his mouth, disaster struck for France. Hugo dribbled out of his penalty area and went to clear the ball downfield. But he sliced his kick and it fell straight to Ola Toivonen. From the halfway line, Toivonen hit an amazing first-time shot over Hugo's head and into the net: 2–1 to Sweden!

Paul watched the ball cross the goal-line, too stunned to move. What a silly goal to concede, but there was nothing they could do now. That was the last kick of the game. Sweden moved above France in Group A.

'Sorry,' Hugo said to his teammates in the dressing room afterwards. He couldn't look them in the eyes.

Paul knew that the goalkeeper was feeling very guilty about his error. 'Don't worry, you've saved us loads of times before,' he reassured him. 'Besides, we had chances to win that game and we didn't take them. So, we're all to blame! It doesn't matter now – we just need to bounce back quickly.'

Four days later, France faced their rivals England in an international friendly. It was going to be a difficult battle and Paul couldn't wait. He was up against his Manchester United teammates Phil Jones, Marcus Rashford and Jesse Lingard. The match had been the talk of the training ground for months.

'If we lose, those guys will make my life a misery for the rest of the season!' Paul explained to France's new young superstar, Kylian Mbappé.

The Stade de France was packed for the big match and the fans weren't disappointed. It was a real rollercoaster of a game, with lots of twists and turns.

When Harry Kane scored an early goal for England, France didn't panic. It was good practice for the 2018 World Cup. Against the top teams, they had to believe in themselves and stay strong.

'Let's get the ball down and play!' Paul shouted.

He was running the show in midfield. He was everywhere on the pitch and yet he glided across the grass like Zidane. When he won the ball, he didn't waste it. He played short, neat passes until the space opened up in front of him. Then he used his vision to create goalscoring chances for the strikers. France were 2–1 up by half-time.

Their lead didn't last long, however. Raphaël got sent off and Kane scored again to make it 2–2.

'Keep going, we can still win this!' Paul shouted to his teammates.

France had lots of possession, but they couldn't find a way past England's solid defence. They needed a moment of magic.

'I'm here for the pass!' Paul called to Thomas Lemar.

He was in the middle of the pitch, thirty yards

from goal. There were two opponents in front of him, but he had a clever plan.

England expected Paul to control the ball and then shoot. He was 'Pogboom', after all. But instead, he played a brilliant first-time, defence-splitting pass to Kylian.

The fans were on their feet, holding their breath. With one amazing touch, France were through on goal. Kylian passed to Ousmane Dembélé, who shot low into the bottom corner. 3–2! The players celebrated together in a big team huddle.

'What a ball!' Kylian cheered, high-fiving Paul.

Kylian was eighteen, Ousmane was nineteen, and Paul was still only twenty-three. France's future looked very bright indeed.

Paul was delighted with his midfield masterclass. It was a great feeling to prove his doubters wrong. If he could play like that in the next World Cup qualifier against the Netherlands, France would win for sure. But that would have to wait. Paul was off on his big summer break.

His first stop was China, where he visited the

Great Wall of China and his old Juventus teammate, Carlos Tevez. Next, Paul travelled to South America for a charity football match against another old Juventus teammate, Juan Cuadrado. The match reunited Paul with his brothers, Mathias and Florentin – it was Juan and his Colombia teammates vs the Pogba brothers and friends – and it was so much fun to play in the same team as Mathias and Florentin again. When Mathias scored, the three of them did a special dance together, including lots of dabbing.

'No-one can beat the Pogbros!' Paul cheered after the 6–3 win.

Finally, it was time for a real holiday. In the USA, Paul rented an amazing house with his football friend, Romelu Lukaku, and his basketball friend, Serge Ibaka.

'Let's get this party started!' he screamed.

For a week, they had the time of their lives. There were lots of jokes, pranks, photos and, of course, dances.

But all too soon, it was time to get back to

football. Paul and new Manchester United signing Romelu joined up with the squad for their preseason American tour. After a couple of comfortable victories, the matches got a lot tougher – Manchester City, Real Madrid and Barcelona. United won the first two but lost to Barca.

'Are you looking forward to Russia?' Paul asked Neymar after the game.

On the football pitch, the Brazilian superstar was an opponent but off the pitch, he was yet another one of Paul's friends.

'You bet,' Neymar replied with a cheeky grin. 'Watch out – we're looking good!'

Paul turned to Barcelona's other superstar, Lionel Messi. 'Don't worry, Leo, at least you'll be able to watch us at the World Cup on TV!' he teased.

Messi's Argentina were really struggling in the South American qualifiers, during which they had lost to Ecuador, Bolivia, Paraguay and Neymar's Brazil.

Lionel shook his head and smiled. 'Very funny! I'll be playing at the World Cup too, and I'll make you regret that joke!'

PART FOUR

READY FOR RUSSIA

After a brilliant start to the 2017–18 Premier League
season at Manchester United, Paul joined up with the
France squad for the next round of matches. If they
beat both the Netherlands and Luxembourg, they
would be on the verge of World Cup qualification.
Everyone was in high spirits as the squad met up.

'Good to see you, mate!' Paul said, giving Antoine
a big hug. They posed for lots of happy photos with
the fans.

It was time for France's stars to really shine.
Against the Netherlands, Antoine scored the first goal
and Paul had three good chances to make it 2–0. But
he missed all three.

'Keep going!' Antoine said, helping his friend up off the grass.

It wasn't Paul's day, but it was France's day. They thrashed the Netherlands 4–0, and the news got even better.

'Bulgaria have beaten Sweden!' Deschamps happily announced to his players.

France couldn't start partying yet, however. They still had three games to go in Group A, starting with Luxembourg. 'The Red Lions' had lost all seven of their matches so far.

'But that doesn't mean anything,' Deschamps warned them before kick-off. 'You've got to treat this match like any other. It won't be easy!'

It wasn't. Luxembourg defended excellently, and France attacked badly. Antoine blazed one good opportunity over the bar and another crashed off the crossbar.

'The ball just won't go in!' he groaned.

Again, Paul had three good chances to score. The first shot curled just wide of the post, and the second was saved by the goalkeeper. They were both powerful, long-range strikes that would have been wondergoals. The third, however, was a much easier chance. He really should have done better.

In the middle of a goalmouth scramble, Paul had a free header. This was it – his chance to be France's hero again. His header looped over the goalkeeper's head, but it bounced off the crossbar and a defender cleared the ball away.

'I can't believe it!' Paul screamed, putting his hands on his head.

At the final whistle, he sank to the floor. '0–0 against Luxembourg! What's wrong with us?'

Deschamps was furious with his team. 'Tonight, we could have made a giant leap towards the World Cup. You had thirty-six shots on goal, and you couldn't score a single one? What a waste!'

With two games to go, France were only one point ahead of Sweden. They had made life hard for themselves.

'Belgium have qualified for the World Cup already!' Paul groaned, looking at the happy texts and photos from Romelu and Marouane Fellaini.

It was impossible not to feel jealous. The France players still had plenty of work to do before they could start dreaming about Russia.

*

In a Champions League match against FC Basel, Paul made a simple challenge to intercept a pass. He was the Manchester United captain, and that meant even more responsibility. But as he lunged forward with his left foot, he felt a sharp pain in his hamstring.

Arghhhhhhhhhhhhhhhhhh!

Paul knew better than to play on. That would only make things worse. He stretched his left leg carefully, but it definitely did not feel right. Shaking his head, he sat down on the grass and called for the physio.

'Is it getting worse?' the physio asked, lifting the leg up slowly. He wanted to make sure that it wasn't just cramp.

Paul tried not to show how much it was hurting him. He wasn't ready to give up yet. 'I'm fine, I can carry on!' he decided, getting back to his feet.

'No way, we just can't risk it,' the physio told him.

'Get a substitute ready,' he radioed to the people on the bench.

Paul was furious as he limped off the pitch. He was in the best form of his United career. He didn't want to miss a single minute.

But the scan results were even worse than he'd feared. Paul wouldn't just be missing minutes; he'd be missing whole months. What would United do without him? And what about France?

'If my recovery goes well, could I be playing again in October?' Paul asked, looking at the fixture list.

The team doctor didn't even have to think about the answer. 'No, I'm afraid not.'

Paul's heart sank. France would have to take on Bulgaria and Belarus without him. Of course, he trusted his teammates to win, but he wanted to be there with them, helping.

'Don't worry. Just get well soon, bro!' Antoine told him on the phone.

With the support of his friends and family, Paul stayed positive and worked hard on getting back to full fitness. He couldn't move as well as normal, but that didn't stop him from dancing.

'Sick moves!' Jesse Lingard laughed in the Manchester United gym.

Paul watched France's final World Cup qualifiers on his TV at home in England. When Blaise Matuidi scored against Bulgaria, Paul jumped off the sofa to celebrate.

'Gooooooooooooooooaaaaaaaaaaaaaaaaaaaalllllllllllll lllllllllllllll!' he cheered.

France were halfway there. Now, they just needed to beat Belarus at the Stade de France. Antoine scored the first and set up the second for Olivier Giroud.

'Yes, Grizi!' Paul shouted, pumping his fists.

It hadn't been easy, but France had done it. Paul was off to the 2018 World Cup.

'Let's go to Russia!' he posted on Instagram with a photo of his teammates celebrating.

Paul couldn't wait to return to the national team. He wasn't quite ready to play in France's friendly against Wales, but he still travelled to Cardiff to see his friends.

'Congratulations, guys!' he cheered.

Paul had a different handshake for each of them – Samuel Umtiti, Raphaël Varane, Alexandre Lacazette, Anthony Martial, Laurent Koscielny... Everyone was pleased to see him, but one person was particularly delighted.

'My friend! My friend!' Antoine shouted when he saw Paul.

This time, there was no handshake. Instead, there was just a big, long hug. Paul and Antoine had really missed each other.

They couldn't wait to head off to the World Cup together.

'There's no-one we can't beat, Grizi,' Paul cheered. 'Russia, here we come!'

MESSI

WORLD CUP WOE

Maracanã Stadium, 13 July 2014

It was now or never for Lionel and Argentina.
After 119 minutes of football, they were losing 1–0
to Germany in the World Cup Final in Brazil. As
Lionel dribbled dangerously towards the goal,
Bastian Schweinsteiger tripped him with a tired
tackle. *Free kick!*

This was it – Argentina's last chance to score.
Their fans held their breath and their tears too. They
couldn't give up yet, not when Lionel was about
to shoot. He had already rescued Argentina against
Bosnia and Herzegovina, Iran *and* Nigeria. His
winning goal against Nigeria had even been a free

kick, just like this one. Could he do it again in the biggest match of all?

Olé, olé, olé, olé, Messi! Messi!

The hopes of a whole nation were resting on Lionel, Argentina's captain, and the best player in the world. He was used to handling high-pressure situations, but this was his greatest challenge yet – to score a last-minute free kick in the World Cup final against the best goalkeeper in the world, Manuel Neuer. It would take a very special strike to beat him, but if anyone could do it, it was Lionel.

He placed the ball down carefully on the grass, pulled up his socks, and looked at the target. He had to get it exactly right.

'Come on, you can do this!' he told himself.

When the referee blew the whistle, Lionel took three steps towards the ball and kicked it with all the power he had left. His shot sailed over the heads of the players in the wall, and way over the crossbar too. The German fans cheered with relief. In goal, Manuel hardly had to move.

'No, what a waste!' Lionel screamed in anger,

looking up at the sky. Their 2014 World Cup dream was over.

Argentina had got so close to winning the trophy for the first time since 1986. In the first half, Lionel's strike partner Gonzalo Higuaín had even put the ball in the Germany net. But as they had begun to celebrate, the linesman raised his flag for offside. To make matters worse, in extra time, Mario Götze had scored the goal that broke Argentinian hearts.

'We were so close!' Lionel thought to himself. Football could be a very cruel game.

In a daze, he walked past the joyful German players and over to his devastated teammates. Ángel Di Maria stood in the stands, staring at the ground in shock. Sergio Agüero was sat down with his head between his knees. Javier Mascherano lay weeping on the floor.

'I'm sorry, Masche,' Lionel said, patting him on the back. 'You've been amazing all tournament. You deserved to be on the winning side tonight.'

But there was nothing that Lionel could say to make his friends feel better. Losing a big final was the worst feeling ever. Only time would heal the pain.

Lionel, however, had to put on a brave face because there was an award with his name on it. It wasn't the World Cup trophy that he really wanted, but winning the Golden Ball was still pretty cool. He had been chosen as the best player in the entire tournament.

As he slowly climbed the stadium steps, Lionel tried to smile but he couldn't. The best he could do was a sad smirk as he shook hands with the guests of honour, including the FIFA President.

'Unlucky, Leo,' Sepp Blatter said kindly.

Lionel collected the trophy politely, but he didn't lift it up in the air. He wasn't in the mood for celebrating.

'Congratulations,' Lionel said, shaking hands with Manuel. He had won the Golden Glove Award for the tournament's best goalkeeper. The two superstars posed for photos together, with Manuel looking delighted and Lionel looking disappointed.

Lionel just wanted to be left alone, but his time in the spotlight wasn't over yet. He had to lead the Argentina players up to collect their runners-up medals. Lots of fans had stayed behind in the Maracanã to cheer on their beloved team.

Vamos Vamos Argentina!

Lionel thanked the officials and let them place the medal around his neck. But as he walked off the stage, he took it off and carried it in his hand. Silver didn't suit him – not when gold was up for grabs.

Down on the pitch, Lionel watched the German celebrations with tears in his eyes.

'The best players always win the World Cup,' he told Sergio. 'Think about it – Pelé, Maradona, Ronaldo, Zidane. They all won it, but not me! I want to go down in football history, but maybe I'm just not that good…'

His friend shook his head. 'No way, you are that good! What about Johan Cruyff? Or Alfredo Di Stéfano? They didn't win the World Cup and they're two of the best footballers ever. Stop being so hard on yourself. It's the best *team* that wins, not the best player. Tonight, that was Germany, but you're not done yet!'

Lionel nodded. That was true, he wasn't done yet. He would still only be thirty-one years old at the next World Cup in 2018. There was still time for his dream to come true. He *had* to win something with Argentina before he retired. Lionel needed to make his country proud.

PART TWO

A FINAL TOO FAR

Before Lionel could start dreaming about the 2018 World Cup in Russia, Argentina needed to qualify for the tournament. That wouldn't be easy in the CONMEBOL group against the likes of Brazil, Uruguay, Chile and Colombia.

Argentina's task became even more difficult when Lionel suffered a knee ligament injury while playing for Barcelona. How would they cope without their captain and star player? Not well, was the answer. Argentina only won one out of their first four matches, scoring just two goals. It was an awful start.

'Leo, we need you back,' Ángel Di Maria told him, 'and as soon as possible!'

It was nice to feel needed by his country. 'Don't worry, I'll be back for the Chile match,' Lionel replied. 'We've got plenty of time to turn things around!'

Chile vs Argentina was a rematch of the 2015 Copa América final. Back then, on that night in Chile, Argentina lost on penalties. Now Lionel and his teammates were determined to get revenge.

Early on, Lionel got the ball deep in his own half. He had his back to goal and two opponents around him, but he still escaped with the ball. It was pure magic. The Argentina fans rose to their feet, waiting to see what their hero would do next.

Olé, olé, olé, olé, Messi! Messi!

Lionel dribbled past another Chile player and sprinted towards the penalty area. The defenders backed away in fear. As he got close to the goal, Lionel thought about shooting but instead, he played a great pass to Ángel. They had scored so many goals together for Argentina. Were they about to score another? Not this time. Ángel's shot flew high and wide.

'Sorry!' he shouted.

Lionel smiled. 'It's fine, we'll score soon!'

Even when Chile took the lead, he still believed in himself and his team. Lionel would make sure that Argentina got the victory they needed.

After twenty-five minutes, the ball came back to Ángel on the left side of the penalty area. He didn't make the same mistake twice. Instead, he curled a beautiful strike into the top corner. 1–1!

Lionel was so happy that he booted the ball back into the net.

'Yes, Fide!' he cheered, hugging his teammate. 'Now let's go on and win this!'

Argentina kept up the pressure on Chile. Ángel crossed the ball to defender Nicolás Otamendi, who flicked it on into Lionel's path. Mauricio Isla was fouling him, but Lionel chested the ball down calmly and squared it to Gabriel Mercado. 2–1!

'Get in!' Lionel screamed as he jumped up into Gabriel's arms.

Soon, Lionel was at the centre of a big team hug. 'Man, it's so great to have you back!' Ángel said with a big smile.

'It's great to *be* back!' he replied.

Argentina jumped up to third place in the
CONMEBOL group. Against Bolivia, Lionel was their
main man again. He set up the first goal with a clever
quick free kick, and then scored a perfect penalty.

*Goooooooooooooooooooooaaaaaaaaaaaaaaaaaaallllllll
llllllllllllllllllllllll!!!!!!!!!!!!*

It was a very special moment for Lionel.

'Fifty international goals!' Javier cheered, lifting
him into the air. 'Nice work, Leo!'

Lionel was now just four goals behind Argentina's
all-time leading scorer, Gabriel Batistuta. He felt
determined to break another record, and it never
took him long.

Lionel started the 2016 Copa América in style. He
scored a hat-trick against Panama and then finished a
great team goal against Venezuela.

'This is going to be our year,' Lionel told Gonzalo
confidently. 'I can feel it!'

After winning lots of trophies with Barcelona,
it was time to win something big with Argentina.
Lionel had an Olympic Gold medal from 2008, but

he wanted more. He wanted to finally win South America's top tournament, the Copa América.

In the semi-finals, Argentina were up against the hosts, the USA. After thirty minutes, they won a free kick within shooting range. When Lionel grabbed the ball, none of his teammates argued. Despite that miss against Germany in the World Cup final, he was still Argentina's best set-piece taker. They had seen him score so many times before on the training pitch and in matches.

Lionel wiped the sweat from his face and took a deep breath. He had a good feeling about this one. When the referee blew the whistle, he curled the ball over the wall and into the top corner.

Goooooooooooooooooooooaaaaaaaaaaaaaaaaalllllllllll llllllllllllllllllllllll!!!!!!!!!!!!!!!!!

What a way to become Argentina's all-time top-scorer! Lionel watched the ball hit the back of the net and then jogged away with a big grin. His teammates chased after him.

'What a strike!' Javier cheered, giving him a massive hug.

They were through to another Copa América final, where they would play… Chile once again.

'We *have* to win it this time!' Lionel told his teammates. The fire in his eyes was burning even brighter than usual.

But when it mattered most, Argentina just could not score. Even with Lionel, Ángel, Gonzalo and Sergio all on the pitch, the ball just wouldn't go in. First the 2014 World Cup, then the 2015 Copa América and now the 2016 Copa América. Three huge finals, no goals scored. It was time for penalties again.

'I'll go first,' Lionel declared. He was Argentina's captain and he had scored in the previous shoot-out against Chile.

The walk from the halfway line to the penalty spot felt even longer than usual. After 120 minutes of football, Lionel's legs felt heavy and tired. Soon, they could rest but first, they needed to score. Lionel put all of his remaining power into his kick. It was far too much power. The ball flew up and over the crossbar.

'No!' Lionel screamed, pulling at his shirt in frustration. 'Why did I do that?'

He walked back to his teammates with his head in his hands.

'Hey, it's not over yet!' Javier tried to reassure him. 'Arturo Vidal didn't score either, so it's still 0–0.'

Lionel couldn't bear to watch the rest of the penalties. He had a horrible feeling in the pit of his stomach, even when Javier and Sergio both scored.

'We're going to lose,' he kept telling himself, 'and I'm to blame!'

Lucas Biglia's penalty was saved and Lionel buried his head in his shirt. It was the worst moment of his life. As the Chile players celebrated another trophy, Lionel burst into tears.

'Hey, it's not your fault,' Sergio said, trying to cheer up his friend. 'Let's bounce back and win it in 2019, right after we win the 2018 World Cup!'

Lionel shook his head. No, he had made up his mind.

'It hurts not to be a champion,' he told the media the next day. 'I've tried my hardest to lead Argentina to victory, but we've lost four finals in a row. For me, the national team is over.'

PART THREE

NO MESSI, NO WIN

'Don't go, Leo!' the Argentinian people wrote on big banners and all over social media.

'You can't quit now,' his friend Javier tried to persuade him, 'not when the 2018 World Cup is coming up!'

Lionel's Barcelona teammate Luis Suárez played for Argentina's South American rivals, Uruguay, but even he asked, 'Are you sure about this?'

No, Lionel wasn't sure anymore. When he had decided to retire from international football, he hadn't been thinking straight. After losing yet another final, Lionel had felt like giving up. That was understandable in the heat of the moment, but he wasn't a quitter. He couldn't just stop playing for Argentina because it was difficult. That wasn't how life worked.

'If at first you don't succeed, try, and try again' – that's what his dad, Jorge, had always taught him.

No, it wasn't the same as playing for Barcelona, where he won lots of trophies every season. In one-off, knock-out matches, any country could beat any country. Teams often used two or three defenders to mark Lionel out of the game. It could be very frustrating when he couldn't find the space to create his magic. And when they lost, a national team couldn't just go out and buy new superstars.

'But I love playing for Argentina,' Lionel reminded himself.

Was he really going to sit at home and watch all his friends playing in the 2018 World Cup on TV? That would drive him crazy! His big rival, Cristiano Ronaldo, had just won Euro 2016 with Portugal. What had Lionel won with Argentina? An Olympic Gold and an Under-20 World Cup. That wasn't nearly enough for one of football's greatest-ever players.

No, Lionel wasn't finished yet. Only two months after that Copa América final, he was back in the national squad for the qualifier against Uruguay.

'Couldn't you at least wait until after this match to make your comeback?' Luis joked before kick-off.

Lionel shook his head and smiled. He couldn't wait to captain his country to victory. With his new dyed blonde hair, he felt like he had a big point to prove.

'I need to show the fans what they were missing,' Lionel told Javier.

'Missing?' his friend and teammate laughed. 'You didn't miss a single match!'

Early in the game, Lionel got the ball deep in midfield. He only had one thing on his mind – goal. There were three Uruguayans around him but after a neat one-two with Paulo Dybala, Lionel was away. He skipped past the first tackle, but he couldn't skip past the second. Foul – free kick to Argentina!

Javier helped Lionel up off the grass. 'Put this in the top corner!' he said with a cheeky wink.

Lionel hit the free kick powerfully, but the ball cannoned off the wall and went out for a corner.

'Next time,' Lionel told himself. He wasn't giving up ever again.

Just before half-time, he controlled a good pass from Javier. Again, there were three Uruguayans surrounding him, but Lionel battled bravely and kept hold of the ball. As he dribbled to the left, he suddenly dropped his shoulder and turned with the ball. The quick change of direction totally fooled his markers.

Lionel had the space that he was looking for. It was time for the magic and this time, luck was on his side too. His shot took a big deflection off a defender and flew past the goalkeeper.

Goooooooooaaaaaaaaaaaaaallllllllllllllllllllllll!!!!!!

'Yes!' Lionel screamed, pumping his fists at the crowd.

He got a big hug from every single teammate – Nicolas, Paulo, Javier, and last but by no means least, Ángel.

'Welcome back, my friend!' he said, lifting Lionel up into the air.

With that goal, Argentina moved to the top of the CONMEBOL table. Their fans started looking forward to the World Cup in Russia. With Lionel in the team, they could beat anyone. But what about when he wasn't there?

Lionel missed the game against Venezuela, and Argentina drew 2–2.

Lionel missed the game against Peru, and Argentina drew 2–2.

Lionel missed the game against Paraguay, and Argentina lost 1–0.

Booooooooooooooooooooooooooooooooooooooooooo!

The fans weren't happy at all. Not only were Argentina no longer top of the South American group, they were out of the qualifying spots altogether.

'No Messi, No Win!' the national newspapers declared.

Lionel rushed back from injury just in time for the big game against Neymar's Brazil. Argentina needed their leader desperately, but how much could he do if he wasn't fully fit? In the end, Brazil's attack was just too good for Argentina's defence. Lionel kept going until the final whistle, but it was no use. With a 3–0 defeat, they slipped all the way down to sixth place.

'We're in deep trouble now,' Ángel admitted afterwards.

Lionel shook his head fiercely. Missing the 2018 World Cup was unthinkable. Argentina's stars just needed to stick together and shine. 'No, we've just got work to do, that's all.'

Against Colombia, Lionel started by curling an amazing free-kick into the top corner.

Goooooooooooaaaaaaaaaaaalllllllllllllllllllllllll!!!!!!!!!!

'Come on!' he shouted with a face full of passion.

All game long, Lionel led by example. He finished by setting up a simple tap-in for Ángel. 3–0 to Argentina!

'We can do this!' they cheered together.

The belief was back. Against Chile, Ángel chased after Javier's great through-ball. Just as he was about to reach it, a defender tripped him. Penalty!

Lionel didn't even think about letting someone else take it. He would never forget that Copa América Final miss against Chile, but Argentina needed him to stay strong and score this time. Under pressure, he did just that.

Goooooooooooaaaaaaaaaaaaallllllllllllllllllllllllllll!!!!!!!!!!

Lionel ran towards the fans with his arms out wide. It felt so good to be Argentina's hero yet again.

'Russia, here we come!' he cheered confidently.

But in the tense second half, Lionel let his temper get the better of him. It wasn't like him to be rude to the referee. He normally stayed so calm, no matter what the defenders said, or did, to him. But Lionel wanted to win the World Cup more than anything.

His punishment was a four-match ban. Argentina only had five qualifiers left – what if their World Cup dream was over before he returned? Lionel was devastated.

'I'm so sorry, I've let you all down,' he told his teammates.

'Leo, we've only got this far because of you,' Javier replied. 'We need to show that we can win without you!'

But they couldn't. Argentina travelled to Bolivia and lost 2–0.

No Messi, No Win – it was that simple. Lionel was now in serious danger of missing the 2018 World Cup.

PART FOUR

HAT-TRICK HERO

Ecuador vs Argentina, 10 October 2017

It all came down to the final day. Chile travelled to the group leaders Brazil, while Argentina travelled to strugglers Ecuador. If Lionel and his teammates won and Chile lost, they could book their place at the 2018 World Cup. But an Argentina victory wasn't just important; it was essential.

'We haven't missed a World Cup since 1970,' Javier said, looking worried.

As the captain, it was Lionel's job to keep his teammates positive. 'Forget about the past,' he told them, 'and focus on the present. Tonight, we're going to go out there and WIN!'

The Argentina players echoed their leader. 'WIN!'

In the end, Lionel's suspension had only lasted one match. But when he had returned for the game against Uruguay, he hadn't been able to inspire his team to victory. The same thing had happened against Venezuela and Peru as well. Three matches, three draws, and only one goal scored. That really wasn't good enough.

Before the kick-off against Ecuador, Lionel spoke to his fellow attackers, Ángel and Darío Benedetto.

'The pressure is on us to score the goals tonight. Don't panic! If we work together, the chances will come. And when they come, we have to take them!'

There were lots of nervous Argentinians in the stadium in Quito, cheering on their country. The players could hear the songs as they waited in the tunnel.

Vamos Vamos Argentina!

'Listen to that,' Lionel said, turning around to face his teammates. 'Come on, we can't let them down!'

A good start was what they needed but instead, Ecuador went 1–0 up in the first minute. Lionel couldn't believe it. It was even worse than his nightmares.

'Switch on!' he shouted angrily at the defenders.

That goal activated Lionel's superstar mode. He was fired up and ready to rescue his team. His clever free kick bounced dangerously in the penalty area, but Javier couldn't quite reach it.

'Great idea!' his friend shouted, giving him a thumbs-up.

Lionel was everywhere on the pitch. If he didn't have the ball, he was making a run so that he could have it again.

'I'll get us to the World Cup on my own if I have to,' he muttered to himself.

Luckily, he had Ángel to help him. Together, they created chance after chance. It was surely only a matter of time before Argentina scored.

Lionel dribbled past one defender and then passed to Ángel on the left wing. It was a move that they had practised so many times before. Ángel passed the ball across perfectly for Lionel to run on to. Not only did he score, but he also nutmegged the keeper.

Goooooooooooooooooooaaaaaaaaaaaaaaaalllllllllllll llllllll!!!!!!!!!!!!!!!!

Argentina were back in the game, but Lionel didn't really celebrate. They still had work to do. He grabbed the ball out of the net and ran back for the restart.

'We can do this!' he screamed.

The Ecuador players had no idea how to stop Lionel's magic. Every time he attacked, they backed away. They were scared of making a bad tackle or looking like fools. He could see the fear in their eyes, and it spurred him on.

Lionel tackled a defender and burst into the box. He wouldn't get a better chance to score; he had to take it. Lionel's shot flew into the top corner before the goalkeeper could really react.

Goooooooooooooooooooaaaaaaaaaaaaaaaalllllllllllll llllllllll!!!!!!!!!!!!!!!!

This time, Lionel did celebrate. He ran towards the corner flag with his fists pumping like crazy. He was Argentina's hero and it was the best feeling in the world.

'Listen to that,' Ángel said, giving Lionel a big hug.

The fans were cheering his name.

Olé, olé, olé, olé, Messi! Messi!

It was great to have their support, but Argentina's job wasn't done. At half-time, they checked the other scores. Chile were still drawing 0–0 with Brazil. That wasn't good news at all.

'Look, there's nothing that we can do about that game,' Argentina's new manager Jorge Sampaoli told his players. 'So focus on making sure that we win *this* game!'

Lionel chested the ball down and turned towards goal. Ángel ran to the right, giving Lionel more space on his favourite left foot. With a burst of pace, he slipped through the Ecuador defence. On the edge of the penalty area, Lionel coolly chipped the ball over the goalkeeper's outstretched arm and into the net.

Goooooooooooooooooooaaaaaaaaaaaaaaaaaalllllllllll llllllllllllll!!!!!!!!!!!!!!!!!!!!!

Hat-trick hero! The whole squad jumped on Lionel, even the substitutes. They had good news to share.

'Brazil are beating Chile!' they shouted over the noise of the fans.

At the final whistle, Lionel smiled with joy and relief. Despite all of their difficulties, Argentina had done it. They had qualified for the 2018 World Cup.

'Russia, here we come!' Ángel cheered.

Lionel and Javier led the team over to celebrate with the supporters. They had never given up, even after that embarrassing defeat against Brazil. Now it was time to party. The players and fans jumped up and down together, singing:

Vamos Vamos Argentina!

Back in the capital city, Buenos Aires, the streets were filled with car horns and music. In the central square, an artist drew a picture on the ground. There was only one hero it could be: Lionel.

'Luckily the nationality of the best player in the world is Argentinian,' Sampaoli told the media.

With Lionel leading them, they could beat any country. Germany, France, Portugal, Brazil – no-one would want to face Argentina at the 2018 World Cup. Not when Lionel was so determined to go down in football history.

✦ NEYMAR JR ✦

HUMILIATION IN BELO HORIZONTE

Estádio Castelão, 4 July 2014

It was all going according to plan for Brazil at the 2014 World Cup. It wasn't their best team ever, but they had two very important weapons – the amazing home support and an in-form Neymar Jr. First Pelé, then Romário, then Ronaldo and Ronaldinho; now it was time for Brazil's latest superstar to shine. All hopes rested on Neymar Jr, the new Number 10.

'I want to win the World Cup,' he told the media before the tournament started, 'and this time, it will be right here in Brazil!'

Neymar Jr worked hard to make his dream come true, scoring two goals against Croatia and two more against Cameroon. Brazil finished top of Group A, but the people demanded more. The excitement grew and grew all over the country. It was the only thing anyone talked about.

'Do you really think we can win our sixth World Cup?'

'If we've got Neymar Jr, we can beat anyone!'

In the knock-out rounds, the tournament got tougher, but Brazil kept pushing on towards glory. They beat Chile on penalties and with minutes to go, they were beating Colombia 2–1. Neymar Jr hadn't scored in either game, but he had helped set up all the goals. He was Brazil's main man and he was saving some magic for the semi-finals.

As Neymar Jr went to chest the ball down, a Colombian defender pushed his knee into his back. It seemed like a harmless, clumsy tackle, but it was a lot worse than it looked.

Owwwwwwwwwwwww!

As play carried on, Neymar Jr fell to the floor, clutching his lower back and screaming with pain.

Worry spread like wildfire around the Estádio

Castelão. Was Brazil's superstar badly injured? If so, what would they do without him?

Marcelo was the first to rush over to his friend and teammate. 'What happened?' he asked. 'Are you okay?'

'I don't know but I can't feel my legs!'

David Luiz was the next to arrive at the scene. He took one look at Neymar Jr's agony and called for help.

'Ref, stop the game!' he cried out. 'It's serious!'

As Neymar Jr left the pitch on a stretcher, he put a hand up to hide his tears. Was his tournament really over? He feared the worst. The Brazil supporters did too, but they still clapped and cheered. They needed him to get well as soon as possible. World Cup glory depended on it.

It wasn't good news. 'I'm afraid you've fractured one of the vertebrae in your back,' the team doctor told him.

Neymar Jr thought he knew the awful answer, but he had to ask. 'Is there any chance that I can play in the semi-final against Germany?'

The team doctor shook his head sadly.

'What about the final if we get there?' Neymar Jr asked.

The team doctor shook his head sadly once more. 'I'm sorry, but you need to rest for at least a month.'

The whole of Brazil was devastated, from the fans to the players. How could they continue without their superstar and leader?

It was the worst time of Neymar Jr's young life, but he put on a brave face. He had to stay positive, for the sake of the nation.

'It's a very difficult time for me,' he told the fans in a video, 'but the dream is not over yet. I'm confident that my teammates will win and become champions. We, the Brazilian people, will be celebrating soon!'

'You can win the World Cup without me,' he told his teammates. The atmosphere in the dressing room was as gloomy as a funeral. 'I'll be cheering you on!'

Neymar Jr couldn't cheer them on live at the Mineirão Stadium in Belo Horizonte, however. He needed to rest, and he knew it would be a nightmare to be so close to the pitch when he couldn't help his country.

Instead, Neymar Jr watched the game at home with his friends and family in São Paulo. It turned out to be the worst TV that Neymar Jr had ever seen. Brazil were 5–0 down after thirty minutes.

'That's it – I'm turning it off!' he shouted as Germany scored yet another goal in the second-half to make it 7–0.

It was too painful to watch any more. Without their superstar Number 10, Brazil had completely fallen apart. Where was the attacking flair? Germany's goalkeeper Manuel Neuer barely had to make a save. And where was the defending? It was their most humiliating defeat of all time.

Neymar Jr's 2014 World Cup dream was over. But the only way for Brazil to bounce back from despair was to look ahead. The future looked bright, as long as their leader was fit and firing.

'We have to move on,' Neymar Jr told his teammates. They were all still in shock. No-one dared to look at what the newspapers were saying about them. Would the country ever forgive them?

'Come on, the Road to the 2018 World Cup starts now!'

THE DUNGA DAYS

Brazil bounced back well after that World Cup thrashing by Germany. In fact, their new manager Dunga led them to ten wins in a row, beating top international teams like Argentina and France.

The problem was, however, that those matches were all friendlies. As soon as it came to knock-out tournament football, everything changed. Brazil panicked, especially whenever Neymar Jr wasn't there. He was still only twenty-three, but he was now his country's captain, as well as their superstar. They relied on him more than ever.

At the 2015 Copa América, Neymar Jr was

suspended for the quarter-final against Paraguay.
Brazil lost on penalties.

At the start of qualification for the 2018 World
Cup, Neymar Jr was suspended again. Brazil lost 2–0
to Chile.

'We need you back,' his friend Dani Alves
moaned. 'We're rubbish without you!'

Neymar Jr returned just in time for the big match
against South American rivals Argentina. The
fireworks before kick-off only added to the amazing
atmosphere. Brazil needed a victory and Neymar Jr
was back to be their hero. What could go wrong?
His Barcelona teammate Lionel Messi was even out
injured for Argentina.

But in the first half, Brazil were terrible. They
never really got going and kept giving the ball
away with sloppy passes. It was no surprise when
Argentina took the lead.

'Come on, we're so much better than this,'
Neymar Jr shouted at his teammates in frustration.
'If we don't improve, we can forget about the 2018
World Cup!'

His team-talk worked. Brazil looked more dangerous in the second half, and eventually, Lucas Lima scored an equaliser. Neymar Jr was relieved not to lose the match, but he still wasn't happy.

'We should be winning games like that,' he told his friend Philippe Coutinho. 'Where's our *ginga* gone? We're Brazil; we shouldn't be playing boring football. We need more 'flair players' like you in the team!'

For the first time, Neymar Jr wasn't really enjoying himself in the famous yellow shirt. Under Dunga, Brazil were solid but unspectacular. Neymar Jr was the team's main creative force, and he was expected to win matches on his own. But without much support, he wasn't scoring goals, or setting them up either.

Neymar Jr didn't give up, though. He had a World Cup to aim for, and before that, a massive match against Uruguay to look forward to. He would be up against the other member of Barcelona's 'MSN' strikeforce, Luis Suárez. It was the talk of the training ground for weeks.

'We're definitely going to win!' Luis argued

confidently. 'You've got no chance now that I'm back in the team.'

Neymar Jr shook his head and smiled. 'Are you sure about that? Wanna bet?'

Luis wasn't backing down. 'Okay fine, the loser has to buy dinner!'

'Deal!' Neymar Jr agreed, shaking his friend's hand. Suddenly, a Brazil win was even more important than normal. There were burgers at stake.

Neymar Jr dropped deep to collect the ball and then dribbled forward. The Brazilian fans cheered; they expected magic every time. As he cut in from the left, Neymar Jr spotted Renato Augusto's run down the right. It would take a special, defence-splitting pass to find him, but there was nothing that Neymar Jr couldn't do.

The Uruguay defender stretched out a leg to block it, but the pass was too powerful. The ball landed right at Renato's feet and he beat the keeper to score. 2–0 to Brazil!

'Yes!' Neymar Jr cheered, pumping his fists at the cheering crowd.

But just as his bet was looking safe, Uruguay fought back. Edinson Cavani got the first goal and Luis got the second. 2–2!

'No!' Neymar Jr groaned, staring down at the grass under his feet.

There was no time for the Brazil players to feel sorry for themselves, however. They had to find a winning goal from somewhere. As always, Neymar Jr was their best attacking option. He tried and tried but the Uruguayan defence stopped him every time.

At the final whistle, Neymar Jr and Luis hugged and swapped shirts.

'So, who's buying dinner?' Neymar Jr asked.

'Not me – I scored a goal!' Luis protested.

Neymar Jr laughed. 'Well, I guess we'll just buy our own burgers then!'

A draw against Uruguay wasn't a bad result, but a draw against Paraguay was. Only the top four South American countries would qualify for the World Cup, and Brazil were way down in sixth place. Out of their first six matches, they had only won two. That wasn't good enough for the five-time World Champions.

To make matters worse, Neymar Jr hadn't scored a single goal in those six matches. He was scoring all the time for Barcelona, so why not for Brazil? Neymar Jr didn't know the answer, but his international goal drought was really starting to worry him.

'Hey, you'll be fine!' Dani Alves reassured his teammate. 'You just need one ugly tap-in and you'll be right back in the game. You'll score in the Copa América, for sure!'

Neymar Jr shook his head sadly. He had something that he needed to tell his friend. 'Sorry mate, I'm not playing in the Copa América this year.'

Dani didn't take the news well. 'What do you mean you're not playing in the Copa América?' he exploded. He was the Brazilian captain for the 2016 tournament and he was relying on Neymar Jr to be their star.

'Barcelona won't let me play in the Copa América *and* the Olympics,' Neymar Jr explained. 'They said I had to choose and I chose the Olympics. I want to win that gold medal in front of the nation. I need to make up for the World Cup disaster!'

Without their star player, Brazil crashed out of the Copa América in the very first round. It was yet another embarrassing exit, and it put even more pressure on Neymar Jr's shoulders. Could he make his nation proud again by leading Brazil to Olympic Gold?

PART THREE

OLYMPIC GOLD

'We have to win!' Neymar Jr told his teammates. He normally liked to laugh and dance before a match but not this time. This was serious. 'Let's get revenge for the 2014 World Cup!'

Neymar Jr was the only member of Brazil's 2016 Olympic squad who had also been there for that awful night in Belo Horizonte two years earlier. When Germany thrashed Brazil 7–1 in the semi-finals on home soil, the whole nation was left heartbroken. Football was their greatest passion.

But it hurt Neymar Jr more than most. Because of his injury, he couldn't be the hero that they needed. This time, though, as Brazil faced Germany once again, he was fit and raring to go.

'They better watch out for us!' his new star strike partner, Gabriel Jesus cheered.

After a long season at Barcelona, Neymar Jr had taken a little while to find his feet at the Olympics in Rio de Janeiro. His goal drought for Brazil was preying on his mind and as one of the oldest players in the squad, his teammates depended on him.

After two matches, Neymar Jr hadn't scored a single goal, and neither had his team. In the next match, Brazil scored four against Denmark, but it was their talented new forwards who stole the show. Neymar Jr was still goalless.

'Don't worry,' the coach Rogério Micale told him. 'That was your warm-up; now we need you at your best in the big games!'

After that, everything had clicked into place for Neymar Jr. He scored an amazing free kick against Colombia in the quarter-finals, then two goals against Honduras in the semi-finals. He had rediscovered his *ginga* rhythm, his Brazilian flair, just in time.

'That means you should score a hat-trick in the

final!' his teammate Marquinhos joked.

'No pressure, then!' Neymar Jr replied. The smile was back on his face.

In the Olympic final, Brazil faced Germany once again. This time, Manuel Neuer wasn't in goal, but Neymar Jr was still expecting a very difficult match. Nearly 60,000 fans were there in the famous Maracanã Stadium to cheer on their country. The noise and colour were incredible. Wearing the yellow shirts and waving yellow-and-green flags, the Brazilians were ready for a party.

Neymar Jr stood with his hand on his heart and sang the national anthem loudly. He was so proud to represent his nation and he was one win away from making everyone very happy. He couldn't wait.

Midway through the first half, Brazil won a free kick just outside the penalty area. It was a perfect opportunity for Neymar Jr. He placed the ball down, stepped back and took a long, deep breath. Then he curled the ball powerfully towards the top corner. It was too quick and high for the goalkeeper to save. The shot hit the underside of the crossbar and bounced down into the back of the net.

Goooooooooooooooooooooooaaaaaaaaaaaaaaalllllll
lllllllllllllllllll!!!!!!!!!!!!!!!!!!!!

Neymar Jr had always dreamed of scoring amazing goals in international finals. He hadn't had the chance to do it at the 2014 World Cup, but now, two years later, he had done it at the Olympics. It was a moment that Neymar Jr would never forget. All of his teammates ran over and jumped on him.

'You did it!' Gabriel shouted.

After the celebrations, Neymar Jr told his teammates to calm down and focus. 'We haven't won this yet – concentrate!'

Brazil defended well but after sixty minutes, Germany equalised. Neymar Jr had more work to do. He dribbled past one defender and then did a clever Cruyff Turn to wrong-foot a second. It was magical skill and the crowd loved it. He now had space to shoot. The ball swerved past the goalkeeper's outstretched arm but just wide of the post.

'So close!' Neymar Jr said to himself, putting his hands on his head.

Brazil attacked again and again but they couldn't find a winning goal, even after thirty minutes of extra-time. The Olympic Final was going to penalties.

'I'll take the last one,' Neymar Jr told Micale. He was determined to lead his country to glory this time.

After eight penalties, it was 4–4. When Brazil's goalkeeper Weverton saved the ninth spot-kick, Neymar Jr had his golden chance. It was like the story had been written for him to be the hero. He walked from the halfway line towards the penalty spot with thousands of fans cheering his name.

Neymar! Neymar! Neymar!

He picked up the ball, kissed it for luck, and then put it back down. As he waited for the referee's whistle, he tried to slow his heartbeat. If he was too excited, he might kick it over the bar. Neymar Jr needed to be his normal, cool self. The German keeper dived low to the right and he shot high and to the left.

Goooooooooooooooooooooooooaaaaaaaaaaaaaaaallllll llllllllllllllll!!!!!!!!!!!!!!!!!

Neymar Jr burst into tears of joy. He had led his

country all the way to their first Olympic Gold Medal in football. As he fell to his knees and thanked God, the other Brazil players ran to hug their hero.

'We did it!' Renato Augusto cried out. 'We're the champions!'

Back on his feet, Neymar Jr listened to the incredible noise of the Maracanã crowd. It was the best thing he had ever heard. After the pain and shame of the 2014 World Cup, Brazil were back at the top of world football again. It was a wonderful feeling.

But once the party was over, Neymar Jr's thoughts turned back to the 2018 World Cup in Russia.

'We *have* to get there!' he told Gabriel. 'If we don't, it'll be a disaster. We need to keep this winning run going!'

PART FOUR

THE TITE EFFECT

After Brazil's early Copa América exit in 2016, the Dunga days were over. Their new manager, Tite, was determined to turn things around.

'The focus is qualifying for the 2018 World Cup,' he told the media. 'That's my job, that's what I'm here to achieve.'

For his first match in charge, Tite selected three of Neymar Jr's gold medal-winning teammates – Marquinhos in defence, Renato Augusto in midfield and Gabriel Jesus up front. It would be Gabriel's full international debut.

'Awesome!' Neymar Jr cheered when he saw the squad list. 'We can pick up where we left off at the Olympics!'

He was very pleased with Brazil's new-look line-up. It even included his friend Philippe Coutinho. That helped to make up for the one piece of bad news – Neymar Jr was no longer the captain of his country.

'Don't worry, you haven't done anything wrong,' Tite reassured him. 'I just want us to have lots of leaders on the pitch, rather than only one. So, from now on, the armband will be shared around. Hopefully, it'll take some of the pressure off your shoulders!'

Against Ecuador, Miranda was the captain and Neymar Jr and Gabriel were the stars. Their partnership was unstoppable. First, Gabriel won a penalty and Neymar Jr scored it.

Goooooooooooooaaaaaaaaaaaaaaaaaaalllllllllllllllllll llllllllllll!!!!!!!!!!!!!!!

Neymar Jr pumped his fists and pointed at the sky. He was finally off the mark in the World Cup qualifiers.

'This is the start of something special,' he told Gabriel as they hugged. 'I can feel it!'

From a corner, Neymar Jr passed to Philippe, who passed back to Neymar Jr, who passed to Marcelo on the overlap. Brazil were playing with rhythm and confidence again. Marcelo crossed the ball into the box and Gabriel flicked it into the net. 2–0!

'Yes!' he screamed, jumping into Neymar Jr's arms.

The Samba style was back, and the fans loved it. Neymar Jr, Gabriel and Philippe – now that was a Brazilian attack to get excited about.

Suddenly, the goals were flowing, both for the team and for Neymar Jr. He scored the winner against Colombia and the opener in a 5–0 thrashing of Bolivia.

'We're on fire!' he shouted happily.

With four victories in a row, Brazil jumped up to the top of the CONMEBOL table. The Tite Effect was really working. If they could beat their rivals Argentina, the players could start dreaming about the 2018 World Cup.

That wouldn't be easy. They were back in Belo Horizonte, at the scene of that awful 7–1 defeat to Germany. What if it happened again? Lionel Messi was fit again for Argentina and he could tear any team to shreds. The Brazilians, however, were full of belief under Tite.

'The way we're playing, we can beat anyone!' Dani Alves shouted in the dressing room. He was their captain for the match.

Marcelo passed up the left wing to Neymar Jr, who flicked it on to Philippe. He dribbled infield and hit a rocket of a shot into the top corner. 1–0!

'Wow, what a strike!' Neymar Jr screamed as he jumped on the goalscorer. 'I didn't know your little legs could kick the ball that hard!'

Neymar Jr was determined to get a goal of his own. He wanted to be a hero too. As Gabriel dribbled through the middle, Neymar Jr made a great run down the left wing. He was unmarked.

'Pass!' he called out.

Gabriel's through-ball was perfect. Neymar Jr took one touch and then calmly slotted it past the goalkeeper.

Gooooooooooooooooooaaaaaaaaaaaaaaalllllllllllllllllllll llllllll!!!!!!!!!!!!!!!!!!!

There was no stopping the new Brazilian strikeforce. Number 9: Gabriel; Number 10: Neymar Jr; and Number 11: Philippe. They were the best in the business. It was time to show off the special celebration that they had practised in training.

The fans in the crowd danced along too. There was a real party atmosphere in Belo Horizonte. Finally, the memories of 2014 were being blown away.

Brazil didn't stop there. They beat Argentina 3–0 and then beat Peru and Uruguay too.

Neymar Jr had scored Brazil's third goal against Uruguay with a cheeky chip over the goalkeeper's head - even Luis had had to admit it was a brilliant goal.

As he ran towards the fans, Neymar Jr patted the badge on his yellow shirt. He was having the best time ever playing for his country.

'You're lucky that you were suspended,' Neymar Jr teased Luis back in training at Barcelona. 'We totally destroyed you! So, when are you buying me that dinner?'

What a turnaround. When Tite took over, Brazil were down in sixth place. Now, they were one win away from the World Cup.

'It's magic!' Neymar Jr joked with Gabriel and Philippe. '*We* are magic!'

But really, it was one big team effort. Alisson in goal; Dani Alves, Marquinhos, Miranda and Marcelo in defence; Renato, Paulinho and Casemiro in midfield; and then Neymar Jr, Gabriel and Philippe in attack. What a line-up! By working together, they were making their country very proud.

The last opponent standing in Brazil's way were Paraguay. Could they stop the goal machine? Gabriel was out injured, and Neymar Jr missed a penalty, but the answer was still no.

Philippe cut in from the right, played a lovely one-two with Paulinho, and scored.

1–0!

Anything Philippe could do, Neymar Jr could do better. He picked the ball up deep in his own half and beat one defender, and then another. He was away!

Neymar! Neymar! Neymar!

The crowd were going wild as he dribbled into the penalty area. There were three Paraguay players around him but not one of them could tackle Neymar Jr.

Goooooooooooooooooooooooooooaaaaaaaaaaaaaaaaal llllllllllllllllllll!!!!!!!!!!!!!!!!!!

Neymar Jr jumped up into the air and roared. It was a spectacular goal, a wondergoal worthy of the captain's armband. It felt great to have it back.

In the last few minutes, a Marcelo dink wrapped up a 3–0 win. Easy! After a bad start, Brazil had bounced back. They were off to the 2018 World Cup.

'We're the first team to qualify!' Dani Alves cheered, jumping up on Neymar Jr's back.

'And with four games to spare!' his teammate added.

Neymar Jr ran over to hug Tite, the man behind the miracle. 'Thank you!' he said with a big smile on his face.

Brazil didn't just take it easy after that, though.

That wasn't part of their manager's gameplan. 'By winning the group, we'll send out a strong message to the rest of the world,' Tite told them. 'No-one will want to face us!'

With three more victories and a draw, Brazil finished a massive ten points clear at the top of the table.

Neymar Jr couldn't wait for the 2018 World Cup to begin. Four years earlier, he had been his country's one big hope. When he got injured, it had been game over for Brazil.

But now, they were heading to Russia with a team full of leaders and heroes. They were the best team in South America. Could they now prove themselves against France, Portugal and, of course, Germany? Neymar Jr was determined to be Brazil's World Cup hero this time.

NEUER

WORLD CUP WINNERS

Maracanã Stadium, 13 July 2014

As Manuel sang the words of the German national
anthem loud and proud, he tried not to look over at
the famous gold trophy sitting a few metres away from
him. It was so beautiful and so close. Manuel could
have reached out and touched it when he walked out
of the tunnel. But he didn't want to jinx it. The trophy
didn't belong to them. Yet.

'Come on!' Manuel clapped as the music finished
and the fans cheered.

The famous Maracanã stadium in Rio de Janeiro
was packed and ready for the 2014 World Cup Final –
Germany vs Argentina. Manuel had lost in the semi-
finals of the 2010 World Cup and Euro 2012 but this

time, Germany had made it all the way to the final. After thrashing the hosts Brazil 7–1, they were the favourites to win, but they couldn't underestimate a top team like Argentina.

'We can do this!' Manuel told the defenders in front of him.

Philipp Lahm, Mats Hummels, Jérôme Boateng and Benedikt Höwedes – they were more than just his teammates for club and country. They were his friends. They believed in each other and worked together. That's why they were one game away from becoming Champions of the World.

Yes, Argentina had Lionel Messi, but Germany had Manuel. In Brazil, he had shown that he was the best goalkeeper in the world. It wasn't just his incredible reaction saves; it was his all-round game.

After his match-winning performance against Algeria, Germany's old keeper Andreas Köpke had given him the ultimate praise – 'I've never seen a better sweeper, apart from maybe Franz Beckenbauer.'

No, Manuel was no ordinary keeper. He could catch, stop, tackle *and* pass. He was Germany's last line of defence and also their first line of attack. His teammates trusted him and relied on him.

'Jérôme, watch Messi when he drops deep!' Manuel called and pointed.

He never stopped moving, talking, organising. It all helped him to keep his concentration for the big moments, the moments when Germany would need their goalkeeper to save the day.

After thirty minutes, Gonzalo Higuaín had the ball in the net. As he dived down, Manuel already had his arm up. 'Offside!' he called out.

Manuel was right, of course. The linesman raised his flag. No goal – what a relief!

In the second half, Higuaín chased after a long ball. He used his speed to escape from the German defenders, but he couldn't escape from the German goalkeeper. Manuel to the rescue! He sprinted off his line to jump and punch the ball away from danger.

'Thanks, Manu!' Benedikt shouted, patting him on the back.

Manuel nodded modestly. He was just doing his job: number-one sweeper keeper.

Argentina couldn't score past Manuel, but Germany couldn't score past Sergio Romero either. The longer the match went on, the more nerve-wracking it became, for the fans and for the players. Fortunately, Manuel was Mr Nervenstärke – he had nerves of steel. Even though he was the last man, he stayed calm and focused.

In the last ten minutes, Germany had several chances to score.

'So close!' Manuel groaned, putting his hands on his head.

But he didn't switch off. He had to concentrate at all times. A goalkeeper never knew when his team would need him. In extra-time, Rodrigo Palacio chested the ball down and ran into the penalty area. Manuel was out in a flash, making it hard for the striker to score. Palacio managed to chip the ball over him, but it went wide of the goal.

'No more mistakes!' Manuel ordered.

He was already preparing himself for his favourite battle – penalties. One on one, goalkeeper vs striker, the pressure, the drama – Manuel loved it all. He had been the shoot-out hero so many times before, for Schalke and for Bayern Munich, but never for Germany. Would this be his moment?

No, because André Schürrle crossed to Mario Götze, who volleyed the ball into the net. What a goal – Germany 1 Argentina 0!

Most of the players and fans went wild, but not Manuel. He punched the air and then returned to his goal line. There were still six minutes of football left to play before he could celebrate properly.

'Stay organised!' he screamed out.

Lucas Biglia flicked the ball into the path of Marcos Rojo. Danger! Manuel had one last bit of sweeper keeping to do. He rushed out, lifted the ball over Rojo's head and caught it on the other side. He made it look so easy.

Neuer! Neuer! Neuer!

It was the perfect way for Manuel to end a perfect tournament. At the final whistle, he ran and jumped onto the growing pile of his Germany teammates. He hugged every single one of them.

'We did it!' they cheered.

Back in 2009, Manuel had won the Under-21 European Championships with Mats, Jérôme, Benedikt, Sami Khedira and Mesut Özil. That night, they dreamt about the future. Now, that future had arrived. They had won the World Cup together.

Manuel put on a white Germany shirt over his green goalkeeper jersey. He wanted to wear the national colours and he was no different to the outfield players anyway. But soon he had to take it off because he had a special award to collect.

'…And the Golden Glove for Best Goalkeeper goes to… MANUEL NEUER!'

Manuel had kept out Cristiano Ronaldo's Portugal, Karim Benzema's France, Hulk's Brazil and finally Messi's Argentina. He was the best in the world.

Manuel raised the trophy in one big hand and punched the air with the other. What a night! He was very proud of his own achievement, but he was even prouder of his team's achievement. The World Cup was the trophy that Manuel really wanted to hold. It was his childhood dream come true.

'Yes!' he shouted, lifting it high above his head.

SEMI-FINAL SADNESS

'What do you give a man who has everything?'
Marcel wrote as a joke in his brother Manuel's
twenty-ninth birthday card.

That was a good question. Manuel had already
won the German League twice and he was about
to make it a hat-trick. On top of that, there was the
German Cup, the Champions League, the FIFA Club
World Cup and the World Cup. He was the UEFA
Goalkeeper of the Year, the German Footballer of
the Year, and he had even finished third in the 2014
Ballon d'Or, just behind Messi and Ronaldo. What
was there left to achieve?

'Plenty,' was Manuel's quick reply. 'I've got plenty
more to win!'

With Bayern Munich, there was the Champions League. And with Germany, there was Euro 2016. They had reached the semi-finals back in 2012, but Manuel was determined to go all the way this time. It was one of the few trophies he hadn't lifted, and it would be cool to win back-to-back international tournaments.

'Why not?' Manuel argued. 'We're still the toughest team around!'

There were two good reasons for him to feel confident as the German squad travelled to France together.

The first reason was that most of his old friends were still there with him – Mesut, Benedikt, Mats, Sami, Jérôme, Toni and Bastian. Only Philipp Lahm, Per Mertesacker and Miroslav Klose had retired. Germany had a brilliant team of players who knew each other inside out.

'I want to go out with a bang!' new skipper Bastian told Manuel.

The second reason was that at the 2014 World Cup, Germany had shown that they were a big game team. They were playing well, and they knew how to play even better when it really, really mattered.

The German fans were feeling confident too. As the national anthem rang out around the stadium in Lille, they sang along loudly and proudly. They were the World Champions, after all.

'Let's do this!' Manuel shouted out from his goal. He was buzzing with excitement.

In Germany's first game of Euro 2016, their opponents, the Ukraine, started brightly, while they started slowly. Andriy Yarmolenko crossed the ball from the right. Yevhen Konoplyanka beat Benedikt to the ball and hit a fierce shot from the edge of the penalty area. It was heading for the top corner. The Ukraine fans held their breath…

Unfortunately for them, they were up against the best keeper in the business. Manuel sprang up brilliantly to punch the ball away for a corner.

'Come on, that's a let-off!' he shouted at his defence. 'Focus!'

Even when Germany took the lead, Manuel stayed alert. From Konoplyanka's corner, Yevhen Khacheridi jumped highest and headed the ball powerfully towards goal. Germany's Number 1 only had a split second to react. Up went Manuel's hand to tip it over the bar. *Saved!*

'It should be one-all,' the TV commentator declared, 'but that man Neuer saves them again!'

When Bastian made it 2–0 in the second half, he ran all the way back to celebrate with his heroic goalkeeper.

'Yes!' he shouted, jumping up into Manuel's strong arms.

In Germany's first four games, Manuel didn't concede a single goal. He didn't have many saves to make, but when his teammates needed him, he was always there. He was unbeatable.

Slovakia's Juraj Kucka outjumped Joshua Kimmich at the back post. His header flew towards the top corner... *Saved!*

Manuel was enjoying himself and Germany were through to the quarter-finals.

'We can't get carried away,' coach Joachim Löw warned his players. 'Every game is a big final now!'

Manuel couldn't wait to face Italy, the team that had knocked them out of Euro 2012. Four years on, it was time for sweet revenge.

'Come on boys, we can't let them beat us again!' Manuel clapped and cheered.

With Bastian on the bench, he was Germany's captain. It was a proud honour and it made Manuel even more determined to lead his country to the semi-finals and beyond.

After 120 minutes of tense football, the match went to penalties. Manuel prepared himself for his big moment. It was his job to save the day for Germany.

'We believe in you!' Bastian shouted, giving him a hug.

Manuel bounced up and down on his goal-line. It was one-to-one, his favourite battle. He stared into the eyes of each opponent:

Manuel dived one way, and Lorenzo Insigne went the other... *Goal!*

Simone Zaza went for way too much power... *Miss!*

Manuel dived to his left, but Andrea Barzagli went down the middle... *Goal!*

Graziano Pellè dragged his shot to the left...
Miss!

It was 2–2 as Leonardo Bonucci stepped up for Italy. He had already scored a penalty against Manuel during the match.

'You're not scoring another!' Germany's goalkeeper thought to himself.

This time, Manuel guessed the right way... *Saved!*

He didn't celebrate at all. It still wasn't over yet. He just pulled up his socks and waited.

Bastian had the chance to win it for Germany. He aimed high into the top corner... *Miss!*

The shoot-out went to sudden death. Italy scored, then Germany scored, Italy scored, then Germany scored, Italy scored, then Germany scored. When would it ever end? Manuel needed to save one soon, before one of his teammates missed.

Italy's Matteo Darmian struck his penalty low...
Saved!

Again, Manuel didn't celebrate, not until Jonas

Hector scored the winner for Germany. Then he sprinted towards his teammates.

'You did it, Manu!' Bastian cheered. 'You're our hero!'

After all that excitement, Germany were through to the semi-finals again. This time, they were up against the host nation France, with superstars like Paul Pogba and Antoine Griezmann.

With the home crowd cheering them on, France attacked and attacked. They wanted revenge after losing on penalties in the World Cup 2014 quarter-final.

Griezmann dribbled into the penalty area and aimed low. Manuel got down quickly to deal with the danger. *Saved!*

Pogba curled a ferocious free kick over the wall. Not only did Manuel stop it; he caught it. *Saved!*

It was going to take something very special to beat Germany's keeper. That turned out to be a perfect Griezmann penalty just before half-time.

In the second half, France just had too much energy for them. Pogba beat Shkodran Mustafi and chipped a teasing cross into the box.

Manuel managed to clear the ball away from Olivier Giroud, but it fell straight to Griezmann. He scored through the keeper's legs. Nutmeg!

'Foul!' Manuel cried out in desperation, but the referee shook his head. 2–0.

At the final whistle, Manuel threw his gloves and shirt down on the grass. Germany's Euro 2016 was over.

'I'm sorry,' Jérôme said, as he limped off the pitch. 'We let you down today.'

Manuel was devastated, but he put an arm around his friend's shoulder. 'No, you didn't. You win some, you lose some. It's not always fair, but that's football. We lost here tonight, so now we have to go and win the 2018 World Cup!'

PART THREE

CAPTAIN MANUEL

No country had won back-to-back World Cups since Pelé's Brazil. That was nearly sixty years ago. Despite the disappointment of Euro 2016, Manuel still believed that Germany could do it.

'Why not?' Manuel argued. 'We're still the toughest team around!'

They had a bit of rebuilding to do first, however. Bastian had retired from international football after the defeat to France. So, who would be the next captain of Germany? There was really only one man for the job. The man who had captained his country through most of Euro 2016 anyway: Manuel.

'He has everything that I want from a captain,'

coach Joachim Löw explained to the media. 'As well as being a great player, he is a team player, a leader and a role model.'

At first, Manuel was too proud for words. Captain of Germany! It was beyond his wildest dreams as a young boy in Gelsenkirchen. But eventually, he had to speak.

'It's a huge honour for me, of course, but we need lots of leaders on the pitch if we're going to succeed,' he said modestly.

To really 'succeed', Germany would need to win the 2018 World Cup in Russia. But Manuel put that goal to the back of his mind for now. First, they needed to qualify.

Germany were in Group C, against…

…Northern Ireland…

…Czech Republic…

…Norway…

…Azerbaijan…

…and San Marino.

Only the top team would automatically go through to the tournament.

'Well, let's make sure that's us then!' Manuel told his teammates.

Germany started with a tricky trip to Norway. Apart from Bastian, all the old familiar faces were there by his side. That made Manuel's new responsibility much easier.

'I don't need to tell you what to do,' he joked with midfielders Sami and Mesut. 'You're old enough to work it out for yourselves!'

'I bet you'll still be ordering us defenders around, though, right?' Mats interrupted.

'Of course,' Manuel said with a smile. 'That's my job!'

Thomas Müller gave Germany the lead after fifteen minutes. In his goal, Manuel jumped up and punched the air. Their road to the 2018 World Cup had begun!

For most of the match, Manuel was just a spectator, but he kept himself busy. When Norway tried a ball over the top, he was on to it in a flash. He beat the striker to the ball and calmly cleared it downfield. Job done.

In the second half, Benedikt gave him a difficult back pass to deal with. Most goalkeepers would have panicked, but not Manuel. As the Norway striker rushed in for the tackle, he fooled him with a Cruyff Turn.

Olé!

The fans loved his silky skills, but Manuel never did anything just for show. All his tricks and flicks helped to drive his team forward on the attack. It was all about winning.

Germany were expecting a tougher test in their next match against the Czech Republic, but it didn't turn out that way. Two games played, six goals scored, zero goals conceded.

'Those numbers make me happy!' Manuel said, looking at the Group C table with Mats. 'Ten clean sheets – that's what I'm aiming for!'

Against Northern Ireland, they made it three out of three. Manuel waited for the danger, but it never arrived.

'Look, your kit doesn't even need a wash,' Sami teased him. 'Maybe we should stop working so hard and give you something to do!'

Manuel had a better idea, 'Or maybe I should just play outfield and–'

'NO!' the other players shouted together. They preferred to have him where they needed him, as the sweeper keeper.

Manuel was off to a strong start as Germany captain. The team was defending well, scoring goals, and winning matches. What more could he ask for? Qualification for the 2018 World Cup was going exactly according to plan.

But as the squad got ready to travel to San Marino, Manuel wasn't feeling well.

'What's wrong?' his manager Joachim Löw asked him at the Germany training camp.

'I just feel sick and weak,' he explained. 'I'm sure I'll be better tomorrow.'

'No, stay home and rest,' Löw told Manuel. 'It's not worth the risking. We need you fighting fit!'

Even without their captain, Germany still won 7–0 against San Marino. Watching the match on TV, Manuel couldn't help feeling a little jealous of his replacement, Barcelona's Marc-André ter Stegen.

'I wish I was there,' he told his brother.

'Really?' Marcel replied, sounding a little surprised. 'You would have just stood there in goal all game, doing nothing!'

Manuel didn't mind about that. He just loved representing his country and being part of the group. Unfortunately, his national team frustrations were about to get a lot worse.

PART FOUR

WATCHING AND WAITING

Bayern Munich's 2017 Champions League quarter-final against Real Madrid went from bad to worse. First, Arturo Vidal was wrongly sent off, and then Cristiano Ronaldo scored a goal that was clearly offside.

'How could you not see that?' Manuel screamed at the linesman. 'He was miles off!'

That wasn't the end of it, though. As Manuel rushed out of his goal to close down Marcelo, his left foot slipped on the grass. He felt a fierce, sharp pain.

'Arghhhhhhhhh!' he screamed, stumbling down onto the ground.

Ronaldo scored but Manuel had bigger problems than that. He ripped off his gloves and touched his foot through the boot. It didn't feel good at all. Even though he could barely walk, he had to carry on. Bayern had used up all their substitutions.

'Just stand in goal!' his teammates told him but that wasn't Manuel's style. He was an all-action keeper.

As soon as the match was over, he was rushed off for medical tests. The news wasn't good.

'I'm afraid there's a fracture,' the doctor said, showing Manuel the X-ray.

'Is it serious?' he asked. He didn't know much about injuries because he hadn't had many. Until now.

The doctor nodded, 'You'll be out for at least eight weeks, Manu. It's April now, so focus on getting yourself fit for next season.'

Next season? That felt *so* far away! He had already missed Germany's World Cup qualifiers against San Marino and Azerbaijan. Now, he was going to miss the return match against San Marino too.

'Just focus on your recovery,' Löw advised him. 'Don't rush back – Marc-André can fill in until you're ready to return.'

That was what Manuel was most worried about. 'I

just don't want to lose my place!'

'You won't,' his manager reassured him. 'You're our captain and our Number One.'

What was Manuel going to do without football? He didn't like missing one match, so missing months of matches was going to be very, very difficult.

Manuel counted down the days. First, he had to wait until he could walk without crutches. Then, he could get back in the gym and get back to full fitness. That's what he wanted more than anything.

He didn't realise just how much he loved football until it was taken away. He listened to music, he ate delicious food, he worked on his children's charity, but nothing else gave him quite the same buzz.

'I *need* to play football!' Manuel moaned at the TV.

The closest he got was going out on the pitch to celebrate Bayern's fourth consecutive Bundesliga title. He had played twenty-six league games before his injury.

'I do get a winner's medal, right?' he asked, looking anxious.

'Of course!'

As the fans cheered his name, Manuel felt more determined than ever to return to what he did best – playing football. He was in the gym every day, building up his strength again.

'I'll be back soon!' he promised his Germany teammates.

Not that they really needed him; they still had a 100 per cent record in Group B.

'You did concede a goal against the Czech Republic, though,' Manuel reminded Mats. 'What happened there?'

'Did you see it? That strike was unstoppable!' his friend argued.

'Yes, but only if you give the guy all that space in the first place!'

Manuel made his big comeback in the second week of the 2017–18 Bundesliga season. It turned out to be a perfect Bayern return – another win, and another clean sheet.

'Welcome back, we missed you!' Jérôme said, giving him a big hug.

'I missed you too,' Manuel replied happily. 'It's great to be back!'

The good times didn't last, however. After only four games, Manuel broke the same bone in his left foot again.

'Nooooooo!' he cried out on the training pitch. He knew straight away that it was the same injury.

It was a disaster. This time, Manuel needed a bigger operation, which meant missing even more football.

'Manuel will be back in January 2018,' chairman Karl-Heinz Rummenigge announced.

Many Bayern Munich and Germany fans were worried about their goalkeeper's future. What if the injury kept happening again and again? But worrying wasn't Manuel's style. He had to stay strong and think positively.

'When it comes to the 2018 World Cup, nothing will stand in my way!' he told the media.

Germany secured their place in Russia with a match to spare and a 100 per cent winning record. After the 3–1 win against Northern Ireland, the players celebrated a job well done, but their captain was nowhere to be seen.

'I should be there with them!' Manuel complained
to himself.

While he was watching and waiting at home, a
great new generation of German footballers was
coming through. Leroy Sané, Timo Werner, Leon
Goretzka, Julian Brandt – the future looked very
bright and Manuel wanted to be a part of it. With his
experience, he could lead them to glory.

But January 2018 passed by, and he still wasn't
ready for his big comeback. Would he ever be ready?

'Yes' was the answer that Manuel kept giving to
everyone who asked. He was used to handling the
pressure. He was Mr Nervenstärke and so he never
let it get to him. If he rushed back, he might make
things worse and miss the 2018 World Cup. That
would be a nightmare. He was desperate to play in
Russia and win the trophy for a second time in a row.

Manuel just needed a little more time. Time to
make sure that he was 100 per cent fit, and then
time to show that he was still Germany's Number 1
and the best goalkeeper in the world.

KANE

PART ONE

NIGHTMARE IN NICE

27 June 2016

'Why is Kane taking our corners?' the fans cried out. 'We need him in the box!'

The air in France was full of frustration. England's Euro 2016 campaign was about to end in disaster. With a minute to go, they were losing 2–1 to Iceland. The Three Lions had one last chance to equalise. Even goalkeeper Joe Hart had come up for the corner. It was now or never.

Harry Kane curled a dangerous cross towards the back post. The Iceland goalkeeper rushed out to clear the ball, but he couldn't get anywhere near it. England's centre-back Chris Smalling could, though.

Harry's corner was flying straight towards his head...

The supporters held their breath and crossed their fingers. They had almost given up, but not quite. England could still do this. If they scored, they were still in the tournament.

But at the last second, Chris took his eyes off the ball. It glanced off his head and bounced wide of the goal.

'No!' Chris groaned, falling to the floor in disappointment.

The referee blew the final whistle.

Boooooooooooooooooooooooooooooooo!

'England are out!' the TV commentator declared.

Harry crouched down by the corner flag, staring at the grass below his feet. His Euro 2016 dream was over already. He couldn't believe it.

How had England lost to Iceland? It was such an embarrassing defeat, especially after their great start. Captain Wayne Rooney had scored a penalty in the first few minutes, but after that, England had totally collapsed. They made silly mistakes in defence, and Iceland fought back to win.

'What a nightmare!' Harry muttered to himself.

He felt like he had let his whole country down. As England's Number 9, he was supposed to score goals. That was his job. But when they needed him most, Harry had failed. In his head, he replayed his chances in the match – one shot blazed over the bar, one vicious volley saved by the keeper, and one awful free kick. That was it.

There had been such high hopes ahead of the tournament. Harry arrived in France after scoring twenty-eight goals for his club, Tottenham Hotspur. He was the top goalscorer in the whole of the Premier League. Harry's big dream was to fire England to glory, but at Euro 2016, he hadn't scored a single goal. Not one.

'Chin up, mate,' Wayne said, putting an arm around Harry. 'You'll have better days in an England shirt, I promise.'

Harry hoped that was true, but what if it wasn't? Manager Roy Hodgson had other options up front. When he had taken Harry off at half-time in the group match against Wales, Daniel Sturridge and

Jamie Vardy came on and scored the goals – the goals that Harry was meant to score.

If only his legs hadn't been so tired. After a long season, Harry's superpower was gone. He knew exactly where the goal was, but the ball just wouldn't go in. It was so frustrating.

'Don't be too hard on yourself,' Hodgson told him. The England manager was trying to lift the gloomy atmosphere in the dressing room. 'That was your first international tournament. Remember, you only made your England debut last year!'

Harry was still just twenty-two years old. His rapid rise made it easy to forget just how far he had come. Only a few years earlier, he had been playing on loan for Leyton Orient, Millwall, Norwich City and then Leicester City. Just when it looked like Harry would never make it at his beloved Tottenham, he had proven everyone wrong.

Now, it was time to do the same for England. First, Harry had to make the Number Nine shirt his own. There was only one way to do that – by scoring lots of goals. Then, Harry had to make up for that nightmare in Nice. Again, there was only one way to do that – by leading England to glory.

'Russia 2018,' Harry's friend and Tottenham teammate Dele Alli said with excitement. 'That's going to be our tournament!'

But first, England needed to qualify. They were drawn in Group F against Slovakia, Scotland, Slovenia, Lithuania and Malta.

'Let's do this!' Harry told his teammates. He couldn't wait to get started on his road to the World Cup.

PART TWO

SIDELINED

England's World Cup adventure started with a tough away trip to Slovakia. Harry was determined to impress the new national team manager, Sam Allardyce.

'I *have* to score today!' he said in the dressing room before kick-off. Harry was so anxious that he could barely sit still. His teammates were surprised; he was usually so calm.

'Just don't think about it,' Wayne told him. 'If you play your natural game, the goals will come. You're our fox in the box!'

Harry nodded and tried to relax a little. He always listened carefully to his captain's advice. Wayne was speaking from experience. Back at Euro 2004, he had been England's new star striker, so he knew all about the pressure and how to handle it.

Proudly wearing the Number 9 shirt, Harry made life as difficult as possible for the Slovakian defence. He held the ball up well and set up good goalscoring chances for Raheem Sterling and Adam Lallana. Unfortunately, Harry didn't get any good goalscoring chances of his own.

With ten minutes left, he looked over at the bench and saw Daniel Sturridge getting ready to come on. It was still 0–0, so Harry hoped that Allardyce was sending on an extra striker to shoot for victory. But no, when the fourth official held up the number of the player coming off, it was Harry's Number 9.

'Well done, lad,' Allardyce said, patting him on the back.

It was another international game without a goal. Harry was very disappointed to leave the field, but he tried not to let it show. He was a team player and he had to respect his manager's decision.

When Adam scored a last-minute winner, Harry celebrated with the other substitutes. He was delighted to get off to a strong start, but he couldn't help feeling a little bit jealous. Harry wanted to be England's goal hero so much.

By the time they played their next qualifier, England had another new manager, Gareth Southgate. Harry was excited because he had played under Southgate before, for the Under-21s. Gareth was a huge fan of Harry's talent and work-rate.

'You'll be the first name on the teamsheet now,' Harry's brother Charlie joked. 'What a teacher's pet!'

But in the end, Harry wasn't even on the teamsheet for that match against Malta. He was sidelined with an injury. While playing for Tottenham, he had run across to block the Sunderland centre-back. As he slid in for the tackle, his left ankle twisted in the turf.

'Argghhh!' he screamed as he lay down on the grass.

He tried to stay calm, but it felt like really bad news. As he waved for the physio, the pain got worse and worse. White Hart Lane went quiet.

Harry tried to get up and play on but that wasn't possible. He hobbled over to the touchline and sat down again. Harry's match was over. The Spurs fans clapped their hero as he was carried down the tunnel on a stretcher.

'There's good news and there's bad news,' the doctor told him after the X-rays. 'The good news is that there's no fracture. The bad news is that there's ligament damage.'

Harry wasn't a medical expert, but he knew that 'ligament damage' meant no football for a while.

'How long will I be out of action?' he asked, fearing a big number.

'Prepare yourself for eight weeks out, but hopefully it won't be that long.'

Eight weeks! Harry couldn't be out for that long. Tottenham needed him, and so did England.

'Who's going to get all the goals now?' he asked.

'Without you hogging all the chances, I'll score loads more!' Dele replied, trying to lift his friend's spirits.

Harry hated watching England play without him.

In the Malta game, wearing the Number 9 shirt, Daniel steered a brilliant header into the bottom corner. 1–0! He was making the most of his chance to impress.

'That should have been me!' Harry thought to himself bitterly.

Dele scored the second goal to wrap up a comfortable win. England seemed to be doing pretty well without Harry.

But a few days later, they struggled against Slovenia. Daniel, Dele, Wayne, Theo Walcott, Jesse Lingard, Marcus Rashford, Andros Townsend – they all tried, but no-one could get the ball in the net. The match finished 0–0.

'See, we need our star striker back!' Harry's girlfriend Katie told him, trying to cheer him up.

It worked. Harry returned to the gym and focused on recovering as quickly as possible. England had more big games coming up, and he really didn't want to miss them.

Thanks to lots of hard work, Harry was fit enough to make the bench against Scotland. But when

Southgate took Daniel off with twenty minutes to go, he sent on Jamie Vardy instead.

'I'm sorry, but it wasn't worth risking you today,' his manager explained to him afterwards. 'We were already winning 3–0!'

Harry knew that Southgate was trying to protect him, but he just wanted to play for England again. It felt like years since he'd worn the Three Lions on his shirt. He missed that proud feeling of representing his country, and the next World Cup qualifier was months away.

'We need you at Tottenham too, you know,' Dele reminded him. 'We've got a Premier League title to win!'

Harry scored goal after goal for Spurs but when England's next match came around, against Lithuania, he was sidelined again. It was such bad luck. He had suffered the same injury on the same ankle, but at least it wasn't as serious as the last time.

'It's only a few weeks,' he kept telling himself, trying to stay positive.

The problem was that the competition for Harry's

Number 9 shirt was building. Not only did he have Daniel and Jamie breathing down his neck, but now his childhood hero, Jermain Defoe, was back in the national team too. Jermain and Jamie scored the goals to defeat Lithuania.

England were still unbeaten in Group F and four points clear at the top. Harry who?

'I *have* to play the next game!' Harry told Katie. 'Otherwise, I'll never get back into the team.'

That next game was away, another match against their British rivals Scotland. Another victory would put England in a brilliant position to qualify for the 2018 World Cup.

'I wouldn't miss it for the world!' Harry told Southgate confidently.

PART THREE

BACK ON THE SCORESHEET

In front of a packed and cheering crowd, the England team walked out onto the pitch at Hampden Park, in Glasgow, Scotland. There were lots of familiar faces in the line-up – Joe Hart in goal, Gary Cahill in defence, Adam Lallana in midfield. But England were led by a new captain – Harry.

'His mentality is excellent,' Southgate told the media before the match. 'Harry wants to be one of the best in the world, and he wants to lead. We need leaders and I'm confident that he can handle the responsibility.'

What an honour! Harry still couldn't believe that he was wearing the captain's armband for England. It was a very proud day, and a very important day too. He had to prove that Southgate was right to believe in him.

It was a surprise and a gamble. Harry hadn't played for his country in nine months, and he hadn't scored for his country in over a year. Now, against Scotland, Harry was expected to lead England from the front, and score.

'Come on, lads!' he cheered.

Harry was in the best goalscoring form of his life. He had finished the Premier League campaign in style, with seven goals in his last two games for Tottenham. His record for the season was 29 goals in 30 games.

'That means you should score in every game you play,' his brother Charlie teased him. 'No pressure!'

Harry just hoped that he would get a good chance against Scotland. If he did, he would take it for sure.

It didn't work out that way, though. When Adam crossed the ball to him, Harry swung his leg at the ball but all he kicked was air. What a miss!

'No!' he screamed with his head in his hands. He could hear the Scottish fans laughing at him.

Harry didn't let it get to him. He couldn't, not now

that he was England captain. He had to keep going.
A few minutes later, Scotland's keeper Craig Gordon
headed the ball straight to him. He was a long way
from goal but if anyone could score it, Harry could. He
lifted the ball over Gordon, but a defender cleared it
off the line.

'The goal is coming, lads!' Harry shouted.

It was substitute Alex Oxlade-Chamberlain who
scored it in the middle of the second half. Harry
breathed a small sigh of relief. They were off the mark
in his first game as England captain. Now, they just
needed to hold on for victory.

'Keep your concentration!' Harry told his teammates.

But with time running out, Leigh Griffiths scored
two amazing free kicks to give Scotland the lead. The
Hampden Park crowd roared.

As Harry turned and watched Griffiths kick the ball
into the top corner for the second time, his heart sank.
In his first match as captain, England were losing to
their British rivals. Was he a curse? Were the team
better off without him? No, Harry couldn't think like
that. England needed him to be their hero and he

didn't have long to do it.

As Raheem floated in a hopeful cross from the left, Scotland's defenders thought they had it covered. But for the first time in the match, they had forgotten about Harry.

He followed the flight of the ball carefully like a predator. This time, he couldn't mess it up. As it dropped in front of him, Harry went for a cool side-foot volley. The keeper had no chance. 2–2!

Gooooooooooooooaaaaaaaaalllllllllllllllllllll!!!!!!!!!!!!!!!

What a moment. Harry ran towards the corner flag and jumped up in the air.

'Yes, H!' Kyle Walker screamed, giving him a big hug.

Harry was always scoring big goals in big games for Tottenham, and now he was doing it for England too. They hadn't won the game against Scotland, but every point took them closer to the 2018 World Cup. He was back on the scoresheet, doing what Number 9s were supposed to do.

'You're a born leader,' Southgate told him after the match. 'That's why I gave you the captain's armband.'

Whenever Harry started scoring, he couldn't stop. England's next match was a friendly against Euro 2016 finalists France, and it only took Harry nine minutes to score. It was another classic striker's goal. Just as Ryan Bertrand crossed into the six-yard box, Harry slipped away from his marker and got to the ball first.

Goooooooooooooaaaaaaaaalllllllllllllllllll!!!!!!!!!!!!!!

He made scoring look so easy. Harry was really enjoying his new role as England's leader. Early in the second-half, Dele was fouled in the box. Penalty!

France's goalkeeper was Hugo Lloris, Harry's Tottenham teammate. They had practised penalties together so many times in training. On his line, Hugo danced from side to side, trying to put him off. Did he already know which way Harry would go? No. Hugo dived to his right, and he smashed it down the middle.

Goooooooooooooaaaaaaaaalllllllllllllllllll!!!!!!!!!!!!!!

Harry was on fire. 'I wish Euro 2016 was *this* summer!' he joked with Dele.

'I know, but at least the World Cup is only next summer now!' his friend replied.

In the end, Paul Pogba inspired France to a 3–2 victory in that game, but there were lots of positive signs for England. Most importantly, they had found their star striker.

But would Harry also be England's leader? Southgate gave the captaincy back to Jordan Henderson when he returned from injury.

'We need lots of leaders out there on the pitch,' the manager explained.

Harry didn't mind; he was just focused on scoring for his country. After another goalless August, he hoped that the dark days were behind him.

'Don't worry, I've got this,' he joked with his teammates. 'It's September now!'

Harry still had to show lots of patience against Malta, though. England's attackers tried and tried, but they couldn't find a way through the defence. At half-time, it was still 0–0.

'We just have to keep doing what we're doing,' Harry said in the dressing room. 'They'll get tired in the second half and then we'll score.'

He was right. As Dele twisted and turned on the

edge of the penalty area, he spotted Harry's clever run into space. Harry took one touch to control the ball and then blasted his shot past the keeper.

Goooooooooooooaaaaaaaaalllllllllllllllllll!!!!!!!!!!!!!!!

What a relief! Harry ran straight over to celebrate with Dele.

'Finally!' he cheered. 'Thanks for the pass.'

In the last ten minutes, the floodgates opened. Harry set up one goal for Danny Welbeck and then scored a second of his own to make it 4–0.

'That's five goals in three games for me!' he told Marcus proudly.

Despite scoring so many goals for club and country, Harry still remembered every single one. They were all special moments.

'Surely, we can start thinking about Russia now!' Dele said after the win.

Harry shook his head. 'We're not there yet.'

But after beating Slovakia 2–1, England were very nearly there. With one more victory, Harry and his teammates could book their place at the 2018 World Cup.

PART FOUR

JOB DONE!

5 October 2017

In the Wembley tunnel, Harry closed his eyes and soaked up the amazing atmosphere. He was back at the home of football, the stadium where he had first achieved his childhood dream of playing for England. England vs Lithuania, 19 March 2015 – he remembered it like it was yesterday. He had scored that day and now, against Slovenia, he needed to do it again. As England's Number 9, it was his job to shoot them to the World Cup.

'Come on, lads!' Harry called out to his teammates.

He was England's captain again, and this time, the armband was his to keep. It was a real honour to lead friends like Joe, Kyle, Eric, Raheem and Marcus. With a victory over Slovenia, they would all be on their way to the biggest tournament of their lives in Russia.

'If you get a chance, test the keeper,' Harry said to Raheem and Marcus, his partners in attack. 'I'll be there for the rebound!'

September 2017 had been another amazing goalscoring month for Harry, his best-ever. He had scored thirteen goals in only eight games for club and country. Even Lionel Messi and Cristiano Ronaldo couldn't beat a record like that.

Harry could score every type of goal – tap-ins, headers, one-on-ones, long-range shots, penalties, even free kicks. That's what made him such a dangerous striker. Now, he had his eyes set on a big October.

But with Slovenia defending well, Harry didn't have many goalscoring chances in the first half. He got in lots of good positions, but the final ball never arrived.

'There's no need to panic,' Harry told his

teammates. He really didn't want a repeat of England's terrible performance against Iceland at Euro 2016. That match still haunted him. 'We've just got to play our natural game and believe!'

But when Raheem's shot was deflected inches wide of the post, some of the England players feared that it just wasn't their day. Not Harry, however. He never doubted victory for a second.

'Unlucky!' he shouted, putting his hands on his head. 'Keep going, we're going to score!'

Seconds later, a rebound fell to Harry on the edge of the penalty area. Surely, this was his moment. He pulled back his leg and curled a powerful shot towards the bottom corner. The England fans were up on their feet, ready to celebrate the winning goal and World Cup qualification. That's how much they trusted Harry in front of goal. Even on his weaker left foot, he was lethal.

Crucial goals at crucial moments – Harry never missed… but this time he did. He couldn't believe it. Harry looked up at the sky and sighed.

On the sideline, Southgate urged his team on.

'That's much better – the goal is coming, lads!'

But after ninety minutes, the goal still hadn't come. The fourth official raised his board: eight minutes of injury time.

'It's not over yet, boys!' Harry shouted to inspire his teammates.

No, it wasn't over. As the Slovenia goalkeeper went to throw the ball out to his left-back, Kyle ran forward to try and intercept it. It was a risk but it really paid off.

As soon as Kyle won the ball, Harry was on the run from the back post to the front post. It was a move that they had practised so many times at Tottenham, with great success. Now, it was time to do it for England.

Kyle knew exactly what to aim for – the edge of the six-yard box. As he looked up for the cross, Harry switched from jogging to sprinting. He could smell a goalscoring chance coming.

The cross was perfect, with lots of pace and bend. Harry stole in front of the defender and stretched out his long right leg towards the ball. Bang! The keeper got a touch on his shot, but he couldn't keep it out.

*Goooooooooooooaaaaaaaaaaaaaaaaalllllllllllllllllllllll
llllllll!!!!!!!!!!!!!!!!!!!!*

Sprawled out on the grass, Harry watched the ball cross the goal line. He had done it! Joy, relief, pride – he felt every emotion as he rolled away and ran towards the England fans. This time, he hadn't let them down. He had scored the crucial goal that sent them to the World Cup. Harry held up the Three Lions on his shirt and screamed until his throat got sore.

'Captain to the rescue!' Kyle laughed as they hugged by the corner flag.

'No, it was all thanks to you!' Harry replied.

Five minutes later, the referee blew the final whistle. Harry threw his arms up in the air. It was a phenomenal feeling to qualify for the 2018 World Cup.

'We are off to Russia!' a voice shouted over the loudspeakers and the whole stadium cheered.

It was yet another amazing moment that Harry would never forget. 'Job done!' he posted on

Instagram with a photo of his goal celebration.

England still had one more qualifier left to play, against Lithuania. The result didn't matter, but Harry treated every football match in the same way. He loved winning and he hated losing.

'Let's keep our focus today,' Harry warned the other players before kick-off. He wouldn't accept a lazy team performance. 'We're unbeaten so far and we're going to finish unbeaten, yes?'

'Yes!' they all cheered back.

England won 1–0 against Lithuania and it was Harry who scored again. It all started with some great link-up play between him and Dele. As the ball came towards Harry in the box, he was already planning his next move. Where would his Tottenham teammate want the ball? He knew the answer. As Dele ran on to Harry's clever flick header, the defender fouled him. Penalty! Harry placed his spot-kick right in the bottom corner.

Goooooooooooooooooooooaaaaaaaaaaaaaallllllllllllllllll llllllllll!!!!!!!!!!!!!!!!!

He made scoring look so simple. Despite missing

four matches, Harry was now the joint top scorer in Group F with five goals. And he was only just getting started.

Now that they were off to the 2018 World Cup, England's real work began. They challenged themselves with tough friendlies against Germany and Brazil. The defence coped well with the likes of Mesut Özil and Neymar Jr, but both matches finished 0–0. Why couldn't England score?

There was a good reason for that – their Number 9 was missing through injury. After the disappointment of Euro 2016, Harry had bounced back brilliantly to become England's star striker. His teammates relied on his goals. He couldn't wait to follow in the footsteps of his hero, David Beckham, and captain his country at a major tournament.

But they weren't just going to Russia to make up the numbers. Harry was determined to lead England to World Cup glory.

CHAPTER 1

CONCLUSION

The Kremlin, Russia
1 December 2017
World Cup legend Diego Maradona stood on the stage and smiled. He was dressed up smartly for the big occasion – the 2018 World Cup draw. There were four bowls of balls in front of him. Maradona's job was simple. He had to pick one ball from each bowl to create each of the eight World Cup groups.

All over the world, the football heroes waited impatiently to hear who they would face in the first round in Russia.

'In Group B...' the presenter said.

Maradona picked out a ball from Pot 1, opened it and took out the piece of paper.

'Portugal!' he read, 'Spain… Morocco… and Iran!'

Spain would be tough opponents, but Cristiano wasn't worried. 'We always knew that we'd have to beat the top teams to win the World Cup!' he argued with his Portugal teammate Nani.

The presenter moved on. 'In Group C…'

'France!' Maradona called out, 'Australia… Peru… and Denmark!'

'I'm happy with that draw,' Paul discussed with Antoine Griezmann. 'Bring it on!'

'In Group D…'

'Argentina!' Maradona cheered happily for his country, 'Iceland… Croatia… and Nigeria!'

Lionel shrugged modestly – he wasn't taking anything for granted. 'Not bad,' he said to Ángel Di Maria, 'but we've got a lot of work to do to win it.'

'In Group E…'

'Brazil… Switzerland… Costa Rica… and Serbia!'

Neymar Jr smiled. Brazil were the favourites to

win and he was full of belief. 'Let's do this!' he told Dani Alves.

'In Group F...'

'Germany... Mexico... Sweden... and South Korea!'

As he watched the draw, Manuel's heart was beating fast. The 2018 World Cup was only months away. It was so exciting, but would he be fit enough to play a part? He had to be. Germany needed their sweeper keeper captain.

'In Group G...'

'Belgium... England... Tunisia... and Panama!'

Harry rubbed his hands with glee. 'Let the battle begin!' he joked with his Belgian Tottenham teammates Toby Alderweireld and Jan Vertonghen. 'I can't wait to score against you.'

Harry was determined to make up for England's Euro 2016 disaster. This time, he would make his country proud.

The heroes had reached the end of the Road to the 2018 World Cup. Now, it was time for the main event. There could only be one winner. Who would it be?

This summer, your favourite football heroes will pull on their country's colours to go head-to-head for the ultimate prize – the World Cup.

Celebrate by making sure you have six of the best Ultimate Football Heroes, now with limited-edition international covers!

COMING 31ST MAY

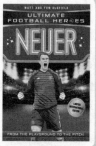

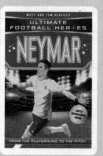

FOLLOW IN THE FOOTSTEPS OF LEGENDS. . .

Bridge the gap between past and present by stepping into the shoes of six classic World Cup heroes and reading their exciting stories – from the playground to the pitch, and to superstardom!

✦ COMING 31ST MAY ✦